In sharing *The Grievance* with all of us – and allowing us to intrude into the cherished last days of his wife's life – Lawrence Abrams commits an act of uncommon generosity. He provides a compelling case for the need to transform a medical system that all too often prioritizes longevity over compassion, and a legal system that is complicit in that perversion. Abrams arms readers with tools and resources they need to avoid their worst fears about the end of life – and loss of control. I commend *The Grievance* to lawyers, family caregivers, and health-care professionals, as well as to hospital administrators, hospice personnel, insurance providers, and anyone else seeking a better way to die in America.

– Sarah R. Boonin, Associate Clinical Professor of Law,
Suffolk University Law School; JD, Harvard Law School

THE GRIEVANCE
A Real Life-and-Death Story

Lawrence Abrams

No Harm Press
New York, NY

ISBN: 0692440135
ISBN-13: 978-0692440131

Library of Congress Control Number: 2015908442

This book is dedicated to Charlie and Dexter,

who later in life will need to understand

the legacy of their grandmother, Sandy Abrams.

GRIEVANCE (from class. lat. *gravis* – heavy) is a <u>wrong</u> or <u>hardship</u> suffered, whether real or supposed, which forms legitimate grounds of complaint.

– From *Wikipedia*, the Internet encyclopedia

~

Over and over, we in medicine inflict deep gouges at the end of people's lives and then stand oblivious to the harm done.

– Dr. Atul Gawande, *Being Mortal*, McMillan Press (2014)

Contents

A Note to the Reader

ON THE ADVICE of counsel, the doctors' names in this book have been changed because the issue is not what an individual doctor did or did not do. It is about a system in which doctors and other health-care professionals follow procedures and protocols that may not be best for preserving a patient's dignity and quality of life. Other names and places have been changed, too. For example, the New York City teaching hospital where Sandy was a patient for more than six weeks is identified throughout the book simply as "The Hospital." However, everything here, including real-time texts, represents the truth as I remember it. I have made a good-faith effort not to embarrass any doctor and, in fact, many of the services delivered by The Hospital were of high quality. Some were not. Unfortunately, because I have decided not to use the real names of health-care professionals, I cannot recognize many who excelled in doing their jobs. It is my fervent hope that this book is a catalyst for changes needed to insure that both life and death have meaning and dignity. – L.A.

1. The Goodbye

SANDY ABRAMS took her last breath on July 10, 2014, at 6:26 in the evening. Less than six weeks earlier, she had been a vibrant 67-year-old woman. She played tennis, golf, and bridge. She practiced yoga. Now my wife of 50 years was gone. She and I had known and loved each other since high school.

What follows are rambling remarks about our life together that I made a few hours before Sandy died. Although she was not conscious at the time, this goodbye was like many other goodbyes said over the previous several weeks. It was witnessed by my daughter, Meredith, and is now part of Sandy's legacy for Charlie, our eight-year-old granddaughter, and Dexter, our three-year-old grandson.

~

Hi Honey

I know you're ready. Your last hours. You have suffered plenty. Now at least you're safe. You're tired, and I want to talk about our life together. You were conscious. You hugged me and told me I was the best thing that you ever did, and you could not have had a better husband. I could not have had a better wife. I love you. It's like half of me is leaving and I'll never be able to replace it. You gave me more happiness than I ever thought possible, and you completed me. We met so long ago, in high school. We hung out in the same crowd. You didn't like me at first but by senior year I grew on you. We started dating. Our first date, I think, was at the Astor Theater. We went to see *This Sporting Life*. I was so nervous when I picked you up on Minna Street, I marched back and forth in front of that church's statue of the Virgin Mary on your corner, my heart pounding, saying I am going on a date with you. Afterwards, we went to Burgerama and had hot dogs and hamburgers and fries, which were considered health foods in those days.

Remember when you decided you loved me because I had chickenpox in the senior year, was out of school for two or three weeks, and you decided you really liked me then, when I came back? We have been together ever since. I knew I loved you when we took a walk in the park. You had your new brown suede jacket, and a pigeon pooped on your shoulder. You just laughed and said it was good luck. Fast-forward to today, over 50 years, and Meredith, coming here to see you, also had pigeon poop on her shoulder. So who knows how things work?

Remember in that senior year when you left in the summer to go to Wurtsboro to a *kokh-aleyn,* the "self-cooking" bungalow, with your mother, father, and sister, and I was heartbroken at the thought I would never see you again, and I went to the bar near Spinelli's pool hall and stayed there until 3 o'clock and got so drunk I was lucky I could crawl home? And sure enough, my mother

opened the door and said, "Where were you?" And I
threw up all over her. But the good thing was she knew
why I got drunk. The next day she offered me the keys to
her car. It was a red Buick. The next day I came up to
surprise you in Wurtsboro. I drove to the bungalow to
surprise you and your parents. I found out you had
another date with a shoe salesman that evening. But you
had the good sense to break it, and from that day we
have been together.

Remember when we were going to college? You went to
Brooklyn College, and I went to Stony Brook. When I
first went away, you were depressed that you thought you
would never see me again. Then I came driving up that
first weekend to see you, and you were so happy to see
me. And then we made sure we saw each other almost
every weekend at Stony Brook, or I would come in.

And finally, one summer, you convinced your parents
you wanted to go out there for summer school. You
could live with the girls, and I could live with the boys. I
was with John, and you were with Carolyn and Ronnie in
these garden apartments which were adjacent to each
other.

Your parents were Europeans. Your father, especially,
didn't want you to go. Forget it. They didn't want you to
go. But what happened was your father said, "If you can
pay for it, you can go," and you got a job as a dental
assistant and also worked at the library, so we could be
together. And that was like one of the best times in our

lives, and we had many best times. I remember Ronnie eating all the food in your refrigerator when you and Carolyn were on a budget. I also remember sitting on the bench at Stony Brook and seeing that shooting star. We figured we were going to be happy together for a long, long time, and we were. Fifty-one years, but who's counting?

I even remember our getting engaged and that giant party that your mother and father threw for us in this catering hall where I knew none of the people, but they all seemed to congratulate me. I remember, too, getting married to you at the San Moritz, when my father was alive, under a chuppah, and we didn't even have flowers. It was sort of a crappy chuppah. But the rest of the wedding was just so beautiful, and we were so glad we were together. That night, we looked over Manhattan from the wedding's penthouse terrace, and the world was ours. We planned to go to Europe for our honeymoon without knowing where we would live when we returned. Maybe we'd have jobs; maybe we wouldn't. We left for Europe using Frommer's *Europe on $5 a Day* as our travel bible. We were there for 45 days, maybe more, and we came back with money left over.

Sometimes there was no hot water in the hotels where we stayed. We went to Pamplona to see the running of the bulls, and we went to the Riviera, and we went to Paris and London. Remember when we even forged the Eurail passes on the trains, and the cops looked at them, up and down, but didn't catch us because you were a really good forger? I don't think I ever told anyone that story. We went through Europe, and you really got the sense that you loved to travel, but you thought this was all the travel we would do. The next year I convinced you to go to Europe again. At first you thought I was crazy, but you went with me anyway. So we traveled, year in and year out, until we had been to 93 or 94 countries together.

I have always loved looking at the world through your eyes. You have a curiosity about people. You can disarm them, talk with them, because they know you're interested. You always ask intelligent questions, and they open up to you and you to them. It doesn't matter what the culture is. It doesn't matter where: In the back woods of Myanmar, or China, or Australia, or South Africa, or Iran (no one wanted us to go there, but we loved it). People just opened up to you. Even the girl, the airline stewardess who met us in the hotel, wanted to find out so much about you. You gave her a bracelet to show your appreciation for her kindness. You were so gentle with everyone we met.

We finally came home to no apartment and no job. They were only material things. We got apartments. We got jobs. We started teaching. I think you came in wearing two different shoes one day because you were so nervous. We loved what we did. We loved to teach. We loved each other. You can't ask for any more than that out of life. Many of our friends changed and grew apart. We changed but grew together. We became assistant principals together. Your mother was worried because she thought it was too much for you. You needed to raise Meredith. But you became an assistant principal anyway and raised Meredith. And when we had her – remember? – I took you in the car and headed for the hospital's delivery room. I took you around to where it said "for deliveries only," and that was where the trucks go to drop off supplies. You never let me forget that.

And Meredith was a joy for life. She was everything to you. You stayed home with her for five years. You said it was a test of mutual coexistence, but you really loved her. You helped her and guided her all through the school years, and you had more patience than I ever did. You stayed with her and made sure she did well, even when we found out that she had learning disabilities and we didn't know what to do. You were the one who was strong, and you were the one who knew what was in her. And you never, ever, ever doubted that she would become something, and she did. She became one of the best people I know, besides you.

You became the principal at Madison High School, and people loved you there. Many of them are coming to the funeral, including Jodie, who you trained. They speak of you with reverence. They speak of you with respect. They speak of your love for your students. You did love them, and they genuinely returned your affection.

And your secretary, Lucille, who I just spoke to, said that all three of you were a "dream team" (you, Lori, and Lucille). They loved to look after you. They find it hard to work with any principal after you because you really cared for them, and they really cared for you and found you to be very professional. And you took a school with a backward, archaic bureaucracy and turned it into something you could be proud of. You worked to improve the kids and to improve the teachers, and you were the best at that. Without a doubt.

You know, some people think living is different from dying. It's not. It's part of the same process. From the second you are born, you start to die. The only question is how you choose to live your life. You lived to the fullest. We know that, and you lived to the fullest with me. I treasure – I treasure every second of it.

Your mother, Edith, survived the war with forged papers to get from Poland to Germany. I think she went as a Catholic or Protestant even though she was born Jewish. I say this about your parents because this is the stock you were born from. This is the stock you pass on to Meredith. Similar stock goes to Charlie and Dexter.

People on the train knew she was Jewish, and they were going to turn her in because that is what people do when they turn on each other. All of a sudden, there was this big, burly man that threatened to kill these people if they turned her in. Finally, your mother said, "Why did you do this?" He admitted he had robbed her house three times, and this is the way he could pay her back for all the goods he took. She did escape but ended up with her false papers as a maid in a Nazi administrator's house, and she stayed there and survived the war. When the Allied troops finally came and arrested this guy, she revealed herself as being Jewish. And he said that he could forgive the Nazis for losing the war, but he never could forgive himself for having a Jew in his house. And through all that, you started to study the Holocaust and your mother's identity, as well as your father's. He met your mother in a displaced persons camp, and she nursed him back to health.

Willie, your father, also was a Holocaust survivor, but he actually was in several concentration camps. I remember a story you told me about him. You loved him so much. He was the one who would come over after school with Meredith and watch Meredith, and then he would tell you the stories you just sort of loved to hear. Growing up, he wouldn't speak of the war.

The stories were too painful, and the *kinder,* Shelly and you, should be spared. But during these afternoons, he was ready to share his experiences with you, and you listened intently. At dinnertime, after Willie had left, you shared them with me. How, one day, your father woke up on a pile of dead bodies that the Nazis had killed and were going to incinerate. He knew he had to get out of there, and he went under the barracks and lived off the stale water. And he made it out.

And in the Holocaust community there is a closeness, to keep the memories alive of the victims of Hitler, as well as to bond with others who shared and survived the victimization. When close family is "exterminated," the survivors form bonds with distant family and friends in a tight-knit community. Holocaust survivors don't judge people by how much money they make or whether their son or daughter is a doctor – well, maybe a little. What they primarily judge you by is how you conducted yourself during the war. And Willie conducted himself honorably. Sometimes selling jewelry for other Jews who needed money to escape and never taking any money for himself. Even though, had he been caught by the Nazis, he would have been severely, severely punished.

Your father then came to New York City, became a waiter, and ended up renting the parking lot by the Fox Theater in Brooklyn. Alan Freed's rock'n'roll shows were his busy nights. He always put his family first – your beautiful mother, Edith, and your feisty sister, Shelly. And you, who never gave your parents a moment of worry.

He and your mother cared for their children, no matter what. And you learned to do that, too, even when your sister died when she was young (26 or 27) and living in Woodstock with her husband selling antiques. Her car hit a tree. I don't think your mother ever recovered from that. But through her sadness she learned how to smile again, especially when she thought of you, Meredith, and, of course, me.

In time, Willie died of a rare lung cancer probably contracted working in a mine when he was a prisoner in a

Nazi camp. I remember your father, who took me in as a son. I remember when I put on his socks when he was sick. He said to me, "That's not a son-in-law but a son." And I was part of that family, and that family melded with my family. My father considered himself part of the working class. He was a Yiddish journalist with Leftist leanings. My mother worked in the Housing Authority. Both my parents loved you because they knew you were good for me. I loved you. My father died shortly after the wedding, but my mother was the total opposite of yours. And yet, our mothers loved each other and became lifelong friends. It was like watching Felix and Oscar in *The Odd Couple*. Our parents taught us the value of relationships. They taught us to value people above material things.

There is so much I have to say to you, Sandy, and so little time. Your life with me, Meredith, Charlie, Dexter. This horrible illness. So much that I want to say to you . . . that I just can't say to you.

I remember what I said to orient you: "You are in The Hospital, in a safe place. You are on the Sixth Floor – sometimes on the Eighth Floor – or at The Hospice. Wherever they have moved you, you've always had a view of the park, so when you've awakened you haven't been disoriented." When your nurses call me at night, I read those words to you. You have a copy. Meredith made it for you so you could follow along. We read it together so you can feel safe. And I know how brave you've been in fighting this terrible disease for as long as you have.

Brave, despite being drugged, in giving Meredith and me the signs that the cures haven't been working. Brave to endure episodes of poor pain management in The Hospital, unlike the comfort you received from the Palliative Care Team in The Hospice. Brave to recognize that you're losing your beautiful memory and becoming less and less in control. Brave to see things with double vision and try to walk when you felt weak and dizzy. Brave to endure the tortures of paraneoplastic syndrome, which has attacked your central nervous system, destroying your personality and, in the final stages, giving you uncontrollable muscle spasms in your right arm.

The doctors previously told us: "Good news. It's a thymoma, a contained cancer." The prognosis was three months of hell, but they said you would fully recover. In the end, however, as the medical journals that Meredith and I researched made clear, you were facing years of rehab, permanent damage to the central nervous system, and possible relapses. But the neurologists still wanted us to believe that they could prolong your life with just one more experimental treatment that had no track record. One said: "Wouldn't you like one more conversation with her? If we do plasma washing, that can happen."

I told those doctors many times that if you woke up as the object of people's pity, with a low quality of life, you would kill me. You were brave and smart to have signed a living will, which guided Meredith and me to advocate for your wishes to doctors who thought only with their heads, not their hearts. The Palliative Care Team met with the Neurology Team and advocated on your behalf. You are comfortable now in this hospice, sheltered from pain. Many of your doctors have come to see you in the hospice to pay their final respects. It is so ironic, but even now you are teaching people how to be in touch with their humanity.

I always ended our "conversations" with these words: "I love you. Meredith loves you. Charlie loves you. Dexter loves you." I would kiss your forehead after I said each person's name. They all love you. People could not help but love you, including all the friends and all the emails that you didn't want me to write (but that I am glad I wrote anyway) so I could share your story and get support. They all love you. They felt you lived with dignity. They felt you were a shining light. They felt you all the time. You had humor and grace. That is how you are going to be remembered, always. In all our travels – in all the 94 countries that we have been to, or 95 or 93. We didn't make it to 100 but we had each other, and that is all we really needed to be happy.

Charlie doesn't quite know how to deal with this. Meredith is putting together a memory box so she can think about you. And Dexter, who you love to see growing and walking and running around, in the end will have very little recollection, but I swear to you now, I will put a book together that will tell them who you are because your legacy has to be passed down. My grief has to be passed down and end so I can get through it. The only way I can get through it is by thinking of you. I will document what people say about you at your funeral, and I will document my feelings for you because they could not be stronger. At this point, they could not be rawer. And I will do this until I process them. I will give those guys a legacy so they can remember who you are and remember our happiness. You will always be around. I love you very much and wish I could have done better for you and that you would live forever. That did not happen.

The only thing I know is that in my life I could not have done better than you.

2. The Texts

THIS CHAPTER contains transcriptions of text messages between me and our daughter, Meredith, when Sandy was in The Hospital from June 15, 2014, to July 9, 2014. For people who have an extended stay in a hospital, time compresses. For about 10 days prior, Sandy was admitted to a medical facility in the Berkshires, with diagnoses ranging from urinary infection to a three-centimeter infarction in her brain.

The ER doctor dismissed her as having a urinary infection that caused her dizziness, even though she had what looked like an uncontrollable jerky head motion. The doctor gave her antibiotic pills to cure her.

Five minutes later, on the drive home, two more jerky-head incidents occurred. I returned to the Berkshires facility immediately and Sandy was readmitted. The next day, her MRI revealed she had a small, three-centimeter lacunar infarction (a small brain stroke).

After the infarction, Sandy scored a zero on the stroke scale, which meant she had no lasting symptoms, and her dizziness was attributed to a vestibular problem in the ear that could easily be treated with physical therapy. Recovery was on the horizon. Her memory was sharp and her muscles were strong and in sync. She left the Berkshires facility with all sorts of advice on how to avoid a stroke. We then went to The Hospital in New York to meet Dr. Jay Frankfurter, a top neurologist, for a second opinion. Shortly thereafter, Sandy developed double vision in addition to the dizziness. Dr. Frankfurter suspected there was something awry in the nervous system. Several MRIs showed there was no visible three-centimeter infarction. Strokes don't disappear.

When I asked Dr. Frankfurter about the stroke, he replied, "What stroke?"

On Father's Day, Meredith and I took Sandy to The Hospital, as Dr. Frankfurter had suggested, where she underwent many tests, first in the ER and then elsewhere.. Dr. Frankfurter suspected a rare disease called Miller-Fisher Syndrome, not the vestibular problem, that might explain her symptoms. Nerves in the ear and the eye are in proximity to one another.

After a prolonged hospital stay, many patients and their loved ones may experience a kind of "hospital fog," and that was so in Sandy's case as Meredith and I struggled to advocate for someone we could not bear to lose.

~

LARRY: In ER observation section   6/15 11:46a

> **MEREDITH:** Almost there
> 6/15 11:48a
>
> **MEREDITH:** Here. Trying to find out
> where to go   6/15 11:55a

LARRY: Don't let mommy know but the ER she was in is called The Geriatric ER. Thanks for a good Father's Day. Love .... Daddy
6/15 2:30p

>   **MEREDITH:** Ha. Love u.
>   6/15 2:33p
>
>   **MEREDITH:** Are you home??
>   6/15 8:10p

LARRY: No. Still waiting for transfer from Er to hospital bed.
6/15 8:15p

>   **MEREDITH:** Ok let me know when
>   u get home   6/15 8:57p
>
>   **MEREDITH:** Is she better with the
>   Ativan?   6/15 9:07p

LARRY: Finally made it. Ativan daze is just what the daughter ordered.
6/15   9:12p

>   **MEREDITH:** Great. Go home
>   6/15 9:13p

LARRY: Soon :-)   6/15 9:14p

LARRY: New single room with park views. Considering moving in with her
:-)   6/16 7:56a

>   **MEREDITH:** Nice. ... How is she?
>   6/15 7:57a

16

LARRY: Fine. Her Miller Fisher
Syndrome is the hospital curiosity.
Hope they are right. Internist Kenneth
visited this morning. Waiting on
Frankfurter.   6/16 8:02a

LARRY [to Cousin Julian]: Got your
message at 11pm. Too late to call.
Sandy at The Hospital with neurologists
still searching for cause of double
vision and balance problems. More
brain scans, more blood work, more
spinal taps. She is exhausted. Suspect
early onset of Miller Fisher Syndrome,
but it could be many other things too
scary to mention. We'll see. I'll keep you
in the loop. Thanks for the call.
6/16 9:14a

**LARRY [to Meredith; no phone for
texting, so this message was by
email]:** Night ended on a sweet note.
Had over a half an hour coherent
phone conversation with mommy about
many things past and
present. We both laughed a lot.
Thought you should know.
Love, Daddy   6/17 10:15p

LARRY: At hospital … mommy
surprisingly good. Sorry for the call this
morning but I just needed to let the
pressure out. I'll try to control myself
better in the future. Luv u Daddy
6/18 9:18a

                              MEREDITH: No please always call!!!!!
                              6/18 9:37a

MEREDITH: Any news? 6/18 2:29p

MEREDITH: Jane's filled in and happy to talk to you and the social worker (if you would find that helpful too). Love you.   6/18 8:36p

LARRY: We just got diagnosis. Doc says good chance it is treatable. If Thymoma, chest surgery will be required. If lymphoma, then she will be treated with medicine. Lymphoma is a cancer but it depends on the type. Mommy did not process that and there is no need to dwell on it. Sending another Doc to see which one of the diagnoses it is. One step forward LUV U...Daddy   6/19 9:18a

LARRY: Spoke with another doc. 3 centimeter mass in chest. If lymphoma depends on type to be determined. Still in grey area. Mommy will stay in hospital.   6/19 9:34a

MEREDITH: Can u call? 6/19 9:36a

LARRY: Long conversation with Sam, mommy's senior resident. It is the Thymus, not Thyroid gland, which is suspect. The prime suspect is the LYMPH nodes. Arranging biopsy to see if there are cancer cells and if so what type. 3 cm mass in upper front part of chest is where thymus and lymph node located. Suspect lymph nodes first because two other lymph nodes to the left and right of the mass are slightly enlarged. Will biopsy the left or right node first because it is less invasive. 6/19 11:56a

> **MEREDITH:** Ok I am going to come up there a little later.   6/19 12:05p

LARRY: Good news is CT scan from the chest to the pelvis did not show any other enlarged lymph nodes so it is localized. Key factor will be type of cancer.   6/19 12:03p

LARRY: Dr. Torres came. Trying to schedule biopsy directly into the mass. Will know tomorrow morning when biopsy is scheduled. Hopefully Friday afternoon. Dr. Torres is great. He has great skills and empathy as well. Frankfurter came in later. Says he is optimistic. Thinks it is paraneoplastic syndrome, not thymoma. In either case, chemo or chest surgery, mommy will have a rough 3 months, but she will recover. Hope he is right.   6/19 5:51p

> **MEREDITH:** Ok.....love u 6/19 5:53p

LARRY: Me too   6/19 5:52

LARRY: May not happen tomorrow. 6/19 6:26p

MEREDITH: Ugh; Why???
6/19 6:36p

LARRY: Give me a call on my cell if
not too busy. Nothing urgent. Mommy
sleeping.   6/20 10:41a

MEREDITH: Tried both cells.
6/20 10:45a

MEREDITH: Call me   6/20 10:45a

LARRY: Going for biopsy now yeah!
6/20 1:32p

MEREDITH: Great!!!!!   6/20 1:33p

MEREDITH: How long does it take?
6/20 2:40p

LARRY: Battery low. If need me call
on mommy's cell.   6/20 4:28p

MEREDITH: K   6/20 429p

MEREDITH: Hi. Where r u? Just left
a message at the house   6/20 8:15p

MEREDITH: How was the
night/morning?   6/21 9:15a

LARRY: Flowers came from Jeanette
and Carl. Mommy still sleeping. We'll
see if she says they are too stinky.
6:21 3:03p

MEREDITH: :)   6/21 3:03p

MEREDITH: Okay got her up. Used the walker to the bathroom. Now taking a poop.   6/21 4:04p

MEREDITH: Going to do the lap 6/21 4:04p

MEREDITH: Took some work. She told me I wasn't the boss of her and that in a minute she was going to give me the finger. Lol   6/21 4:05

LARRY: Meanwhile I looked everywhere and I can't find the ring and earrings. Maybe in Becket but I doubt it. She is going to kill me. What do you know about buying new diamond rings? Sounds like you are playing with her well. Glad you got her to walk. Luv. Me 6/21 4:11p

MEREDITH: She gets a good report. Took then full lap

LARRY: Good report?   6/21 4:21p

MEREDITH: Yes.   6/21 4:21p

MEREDITH: She cruised with the walker. I was surprised Now ice cream 6/21 4:22p

LARRY: It is fun when you see her progressing She has strength..balance is the problem. Try to give her some

cashews first and watch the face she will
make   6/21 4:23p

> **MEREDITH:** Had cashews and now a
> banana. And we opened the blinds to
> look at her request. And she really loves
> the flowers from Jeanette and Carl.
> 6/21 4:29p

LARRY: Good. Do the flowers have
diamond ring in them? Look hard
6/21 4:51p

> **MEREDI**TH: Could someone check
> her dresser in Becket?   6/21 4:53p

LARRY: On it.   6/21 4:53p

> **MEREDITH:** Come up for a quick
> visit.   6/22 1:57p

> **MEREDITH:** Did they find the ring?
> 6/22 4:08p

LARRY: No.

LARRY: Mommy in much better
mood. Took her on wheelchair around
hospital. She perked up. Ate quiche,
some salad, fruit cup and cheesecake.
Watching golf. May have been
exhausted from the night's ordeal.
Waiting for the night nurse to go over
her routine and biopsy prep.
6/22 5:57p

MEREDITH: Ok thats good on getting her up. She asked me yesterday if there was a garden. (After the walk) 6/22 6:00p

LARRY: She is trying to do the times crossword puzzle using her readers and keeping one eye closed. She's getting some answers. :)   6/22 6:45p

MEREDITH: Good   6/22 6:47p

LARRY: Biopsy day. At hospital now. mommy slept. thru nite.   6/23 6:22a

MEREDITH: Sleeping thru the night is good. Any chance you did too? 6/22 6:58a

LARRY: Some but not enough. Spoke with Dr. Kenneth. Feels if thymoma it is benign. If lymphoma chemotherapy and radiation may be needed, but most likely treatable. Weekend docs orders of compression boots and iv fluids … not necessary. Happy its Monday and the A team of docs are back!   6/23 7:16a

MEREDITH: Did he say when they will have the results (and we should probably factor that it will be a day later than they actually say).   6/23 7:20a

LARRY: 2 to 3 days. If given tentative results right after procedure it can be misleading.   6/23 7:49a

LARRY: Mommy using tweezers to groom her face. She cares about her looks. Struggling to remember who has an anniversary on 6/26. No way I can help her remember what I never knew....Just criticized the quality of the tweezers I purchased. "Where did you get these tweezers?" LOL
6/23 8:02a

                    MEREDITH: Ha - you just used LOL
                    6/23 8:03a

LARRY: I'm a texting dad!   6/23 8:05a

          MEREDITH: :)   6/23 8:06a

LARRY: Mommy developed post op complication from needle biopsy. Small pocket of air in one lung from x ray Doc thinks it is stable and will go away by itself. Taking 2nd x ray now. Mommy's oxygen levels good. In some pain in chest and back shoulders. She is confused. Thinks it is lung cancer. Will stay on it with docs and let you know. Asked thoracic surgeon to visit. UGH
6/23 3:03p

                    MEREDITH: Ug ok   6/23 3:04p

                    MEREDITH: Charlie at gap casting
                    6/23 3:07p

LARRY: 2nd xray shows no further expansion of air pocket. Plan: if mommy in pain an hour after Tylenol, doc will aspirate lung (stick straw in and suck the air out). Let you know. I even gave her a Haagen Dazs bar without her walking. She is having a hard day. No need to come.   6/23 4/11p

LARRY: When will Charlie find out if she made it?   6/23 4:14p

                    MEREDITH: No idea. Think within the next few days bc the shooting starts later this week (but we said she could only do the other date so she doesn't miss the last few days of school) 6/23 4:18p

LARRY: R U nuts? Nothing happens in the last days of school. Get your little money maker on the job momma Rose (as in the play, Gypsy). Mommy feeling better. Two Tylenol and a melted cheese sandwich did it. 6/23 5:24p

LARRY: Arrived at mommy's side at 7:15. Air bubble seems reabsorbed. She is not in any pain Ate her French Toast, bacon, yogurt and apple juice so appetite is back. Hope she doesn't expect breakfast like this one when I get her home. Dr. Kenneth saw her this morning and thinks her mood is somewhat better. Had no calls from her during the night. She was trying to call me when I arrived. Sleeping peacefully now. Will try to get her up and about when she awakes. If she resists will text

you to call her. You can try the Haagen
Dazs bribe. Yesterday she broke me
down and got one without walking. Stay
strong!   6/24 8:56a

> **MEREDITH:** Thanks for the update.
> Was just going to call. Tell me when she
> is awake and I'll call then.
> 6/24 8:58a

LARRY: Change of plan... Spoke with
docs...air bubble still not resolved.
Mommy should stay in bed except
when she goes to the bathroom and
takes her spa treatment   6/24 9:42a

> **MEREDITH:** K   6/24 9:43a

LARRY: Got mommy a spa treatment
and cajoled her to walk a lap around the
wing. At one point she started to walk
real fast. Slow down, I said. She
snapped back, I want this over with as
fast as I can! Eating lunch now. Another
x ray to check air bubble. Had a
conversation with doc re mommy's
condition. When he left she did not
understand terminology. I translated,
"They don't know shit until pathology
comes back." She repeated the phrase.
6/24 12:35p

LARRY: Jane sent flowers. Very sweet.
Need her e mail for thank you.
6/24 12:37p

> **MEREDITH:** Did u get the x ray
> results?   6/24 3:21p

LARRY: Yes bubble increased slightly.
Monitor and take another x ray at 11:30
pm and then decide if straw suck out
the air procedure is warranted.
6/24 3:28p

> **MEREDITH:** Ok. I love u.
> 6/24 3:50p

LARRY: Spoke with Frankfurter.
Hopeful regarding Thymoma . It is not
benign but very contained and much
better than lymphoma. Even if spread
to the lymph node behind the thymus,
it still is localized. The shoulder to
pelvis CT scan showed no other signs
of cancer. Frankfurter feels operation
to remove thymoma will cure the
double vision. May or may not stop
dizziness and not related to short term
memory issues.Mommy will need some
rehab for walking/balance. Myasthenia
Gravis set off by thymoma is when
auto immune system attacks the nerves
.. impact on the muscles, thus the
double vision. Dr. Torres, thoracic
surgeon is top doc for this operation.
Need to pick his mind about the
prognosis.   6/24 5:24p

> **MEREDITH:** Running late. Call u in a
> few.   6/25 9:42a

> **MEREDITH:** Been trying to call your
> cell but not going thru. Can u call the
> office - att: Abrams room West
> 6/25 10:24a

MEREDITH: Can you double check fax number. Not going thru. But it may be this printer Think i just got it to send.   6/25 12:22p

LARRY: Got it. Dr F stopped by. Going to test mommy for MG below waist. Above waist negative . Test is called EMG. Docs still searching because low salt in kidney may be inconsistent with MG. In either case thymoma needs to come out.
6/25 12:31p

MEREDITH: Ok....   6/25 1:04p

LARRY: With mommy. Showed her Dexter video and picture. Perked her up. Confused as to dates. Same as yesterday...not worse. Getting spa treatment now. Try to walk her later. Can't eat till after PEP test completed by 3:30. Mommy not happy when hungry.   6/26 9:04a

MEREDITH: Thought the test was 1:30?   6/26 9:06a

LARRY: Done at 3:30...?
6/26 9:06a

MEREDITH: Just got into office. Let me know when to call..   6/26 9:06a

LARRY: K   test 2 hours.... phone in 20 minutes   6/26 9:08a

MEREDITH: Ok   6/26 9:11a

MEREDITH: I am in a meeting til
10:30. Will call then.   6/26 9:38a

LARRY: Mommy in PET scan…
radioactive. Next nerve conduction test
to eliminate mg. Back in room about 5.
Luv U..Daddy   6/26 2:13p

MEREDITH: Ok   6/26 2:30p

LARRY: Surgery scheduled for 7:30 am
6/26 5:36p

MEREDITH: Okay. What time r u
getting there?   6/26 6:19

MEREDITH: Jane didn't get your
email. Resend to it to her.   6/26 7:56p

LARRY: Had to rewrite it on Mac. Mail
server on 1 pad failed. Confirm cc copy
to you. Around 9:30 last night. With
mommy at hospital. She slept thru and
is sleeping now. She gets hot feet so she
took her socks half off. Cute :)
6/27 6:02a

MEREDITH: On my way....
6/27 6:53a

MEREDITH: At a reception desk
6/27 7:29a

LARRY: According to my reading of
the 3 pain meds mommy is taking, the
side effects include change in thinking
clearly with logic and hallucinations.
Fentanyl bupivacaine and

hydromorphone, may account for
mommy's day. Enjoy your dinner and
concert. Tomorrow is another day .
Love. Daddy   6/28 5:53p

> **MEREDITH:** Let's hope. Love you.
> 6/28 6:05p

LARRY: Fentanyl doesn't leave her
body till she pees. She hasn't yet :)
6/28 6:15p

> **MEREDITH:** K   6/28 6:17p

LARRY: Has not peed yet. Drug still
circulating in her body. Trying to pee
now. Don't know if she will be
successful. The suspense is nerve
wracking. :)))   6/28 6:20

> **MEREDITH:** Keep me posted.
> 6/28 6:46p

LARRY: Didn't pee. Aurora, her nurse,
will put in catheter. Not allowed to send
pictures.   6/28 6:50p

> **MEREDITH:** Good bc we are eating.
> 6/28 6:52p

> **MEREDITH:** Dex on a trampoline!
> Drew just sent. Lol   6/28 7:14p

> **MEREDITH:** Are u home??
> 6/28 8:30p

LARRY: Yes   6/28 8:34p

MEREDITH: I love you ;)
6/28 8:46p

LARRY: Luv. U 2   6/26 8:46p

MEREDITH: Did u see the video of dex?   6/26 8:47p

MEREDITH: Just making sure bc it's silly and will make u smile.
6/28 8:48

LARRY: No where?   6/28 8:48p

MEREDITH: Sending it again.
6/28 8:50p

MEREDITH: Get it?   6/28 8:50p

MEREDITH: And he loves dogs Click on the video   6/28 8:54p

MEREDITH: On trampoline. Show it to mommy tomorrow.   6/28 8:56p

LARRY: PS Your text is a little slurred. How many have you had? LOL
6/28 8:57p

MEREDITH: Ha! Not enough
6/28 8:58p

MEREDITH: Going to sleep. Enjoy the concert. Hi to Eric   8/28 8:59p

LARRY: Love you. We both say goodnight   6/28 9:02

LARRY: With mommy. Given some Ativan last night. Tried to get up several times w/o calling the nurse. Sleeping now. Recognized me when I came in. Spoke with kidney doc. Sodium level 128, down from 130. Probably caused by pain meds and liquid diet going over 1 liter over day. Not a precipitous drop so not worried. Thinks paraneoplastic syndrome chemicals will need approximately 2 weeks to exit her brain and her kidneys should clear as well. 6/29 8:15a

> **MEREDITH:** Okay well I guess that is all good.   6/29 8:57

LARRY: Except he is a kidney doc, not a neurologist Just spoke 2 Torres' resident. He is not surprised either. Says antibodies need time to clear. 6/29 9:03a

> **MEREDITH:** Okay. Definitely hoping for that. Does she seem the same (but w no worry)?   6/29 9:09

LARRY: She's been zzzzzz since I got here. Her zzzzzz sound the same. Have not yet had a sustained conversation with her. Will let you know when she is fully awake.   6/29 9:12a

> **MEREDITH:** Okay. I will come this afternoon. Had a very good intense cry last night about all this and my eyes are totally swollen puff balls. Was probably needed. Love you.   6/29 9:22a

LARRY: Testing   6/29 9:55a

> **MEREDITH:** What are u testing?
> 6/29 9:55a

LARRY: Not u fortunately :)
6/29 10:06a

> **MEREDITH:** Spending some time w
> Charlie getting manicure/pedicure then
> coming there   6/29 11:29a

LARRY: Good. Say hi to Charlie
6/29 11:31a

> **MEREDITH:** K   6/29 1:07p

> **MEREDITH:** On my way now
> 6/29 1:09p

LARRY: Mommy sleeping peacefully.
Opens eyes every now and then but
dozes back off. BP 130/65. Doctor My
Father Died I Feel Your Pain (First
nickname for Dr. Gay Schluffen, the
pain management specialist) stopped by
but mommy refused to turn over to let
her check epidural.. Go mommy! Will
leave shortly after Jenny, the physician
assistant briefs next PA.   6/29 7:15p

> **MEREDITH:** Ok thanks. Sounds
> good.   6/29 7:28p

LARRY: At hospital. Mommy sleeping
again. Got thru till 4 in morning, then
had another pain/where am I episode.
Saw Dr. Empathetic (Second nickname

for Dr. Gay Schluffen, pain
management specialist) and PA. Given
1/2 Ativan and Benadryl for pain. See
what today brings.   6/30 6:54a

LARRY: Just saw docs on rounds.
Chest tube and catheter coming out
today. Should make her more
comfortable. Try to walk later. She is
somewhat coherent. Played Jewish
Geography with Dr. Robert Weiss.
6/30 7:51a

                    MEREDITH: Ok. Thank u. Love u.
                    Will prob come up late afternoon "Dr
                    Empathetic" lol   6/30 8:52a

                    MEREDITH: Real hospital today. Met
                    with Torres. Post op surgical prognosis
                    good. Pathology later in week.
                    Transferring back to neurology today or
                    tomorrow. Met with Frankfurter. Said it
                    will take a while to formulate a plan.
                    Mommy still has 2x vision. It may be
                    paraneoplastic syndrome or something
                    else not yet discovered. The search for
                    answers continues.   6/30 10:09

LARRY: Met with Dr. Gay Schluffen
of pain services. Removed epidural.
Control pain by pills and iv if needed.
Asked him to distinguish pain from
anxiety. Made point if holding chest and
grimacing it is pain. Monitoring
mommy for next hour when epidural
wears off. I told him about yesterday
and the failure to get a quick enough

response to her pain. He assured me he
was board certified and had 30 years
experience. I told him I had 47 years
experience with mommy and did not
want to see her in pain again. He got
the point until he started the "in elderly
patients" routine. [Looked Dr.
Schluffen's age up on-line. The Hospital
website says he is 55. His comments
made him seem older and not in a good
way.]   6/30 11:01a

MEREDITH: Ug.. 11:56a

MEREDITH: Ran out of the office
and my phone is about to die.
6/30 11:58a

LARRY: Unbelievable! Watching
mommy. 25 minutes after Dr Schluffen
leaves I see her grimacing. Ask for
nurse. Concerned mommy did not get
oral pain meds as prescribed. Nurse
Loopy did not know epidural was
disconnected. I called her four times.
Called her for 20 minutes ...no
response. Can't stand seeing her in real
pain and nothing happening. Don't
doctors know how to communicate
with nurses. Unbelievable! What if I
weren't here? Called Tova, nurse
supervisor. Gave mommy IV meds. I
insisted on a nurse change Oral meds
should have been given when epi
removed. New nurse's name is Lena.
She is great. Mommy loopy but not in

pain. Finally cleaning her up and paying attention.   6/30 12:24p

>   **MEREDITH:** Is delaudid oral okay to
>   give her? Nurse came by and said it was
>   time but wanted to check w u first.
>   6/30 3:53p

LARRY: Call on your way home.
Love u.   6/30 7:26p

LARRY: Mommy called me at 9:30
2nite scared and lost. She didn't know
where she was and was refusing meds
like Benedryl which will make her sleep
and relieve the pain. One to one aide
called me. Spoke to mommy for about
40 minutes with tears in my eyes. Got
her to accept meds from nurse saving
half dose of Ativan if she wakes up
scared in early morning. As she was
nodding off, told her to dream of you.
It made her less scared and she nodded
off. What a relief to have someone in
the room who can put mommy in
contact with me.   6/30 10:50p

>   **MEREDITH:** Wow. Ok. I hope she is
>   calm now and sleeps. And that you do
>   too. Love you.   6/30 10:54a

LARRY: Mommy still drugged. 1 to 1
in effect till 3. May go to the neuro
floor today. I spoke with Dr.
Frankfurter. Researched and discovered
paraneoplastic syndrome is consistent
with some thymomas. Blood test can

confirm diagnosis. Kenneth, our
primary doc advised me to stick with
Frankfurter because he is brilliant.
Luv U.   7/1 9:05a

MEREDITH: Ok just left you
message. That's the most promising
thing I guess.   7/1 9:09a

MEREDITH: When are they doing a
blood test? And why haven't they
already if just a simple blood test?
7/1 9:10a

LARRY: Don't know. My suspicion is
there is a lot of sophisticated science to
discover what type of antibodies to test
for. This is exactly why I wanted you to
marry a doctor. Last blood work went
to Mayo clinic and sample was lost.
Spoke with Julian and Ro last night.
Offered to help when you are away.
We'll see. Spoke with Marilyn Weiss in
Montreal. By the way, Frankfurter also
confided in me that his wife and
children think he is a bit of a jerk. But
he is our jerk so hope he is right. In a
few days he also may repeat spinal tap.
7/1 9:42a

LARRY: In planning your day, know
that I am in Starbucks. Aide has my cell.
Too crowded in room otherwise. May
move mommy later. Not necessary for
you to come to give me a break. Just
consider your options in planning your
day. Don't want a child of mine to be

37

running around like a chicken without a
head.   7/1 10:15a

                      MEREDITH: :) ok   7/1 10:37

LARRY: Mommy walking yeah!
7/1 11:31a

                      MEREDITH: Oh good   7/1 11:34a

LARRY: Mommy now sitting in chair
having coherent conversation with her
aide in Spanish.   7/1 12:13p

                      MEREDITH: Really?!   7/1 12:13p

                      MEREDITH: How do u know it's
coherent if it's in Spanish?
7/1 12:14p

LARRY: U got me lol   7/1 12:14p

                      MEREDITH: :)   7/1 12:15p

LARRY: Mommy now in a new room
for tonight.   7/1 4:33p

                      MEREDITH: That's good right?
7/1 4:37p

                      MEREDITH: Will she still have a
nurse at night?   7/1 4:37p

LARRY: Think so. Or aide attached to
nurse. It's a good thing. Needed other
room for sick person :-)   7/1 4:47p

MEREDITH: Ok. Still at work cant call til later -- might be too late. 7/1 4:48p

LARRY: Don't worry. Call me later tonight.   7/1 4:51p

LARRY: Mommy had bad night. No pain but drugs made her delusional. Around 10 pm scared and refusing To take Ativan and Benadryl. Talked her down. Called me again at around 12:30. Mommy delusional scared and screaming.
Talked her down to the point she would accept 2nd shot of Ativan. Stayed with her until she fell asleep. Sleeping now. Met with renal docs this morning. Sodium down to 128 but white count count up to 1400.; 1000 is normal. Suspect some sort of infection, which might have contributed to last night's incident. Will speak with more docs today.   7/2 8:29a

MEREDITH: :(ok   7/2 8:31

LARRY: One to one aide in room will continue when Mommy moves to 8 West :)   7/2 10:03

MEREDITH: Oh good. 7/2 10:03a

LARRY: I think from my talk with Frankfurter he feels my urgency thank goodness. MRI scheduled today. 7/2 10:10a

MEREDITH: Well I hope so. This is insanity at this point.   7/2 10:11a

LARRY: Beyond! BC white count elevated, mommy should be in private room. Sending you an e mail soon with Mommy's meds. Blow it up if you can and bring it with you. If she can read it with me it will help me reassure her she is safe, especially if she calls me at night. Luv   7/2 11:02a

MEREDITH: Will do   7/2 11:02a

MEREDITH: How was the night? 7/3 7:24a

LARRY: In pain. 2x IV meds helped. Sleeping now   7/3 7:25a

MEREDITH: Ok. Getting showered and need to spend a good amount of the day in office. Then will come up there with the print outs. Love you :-) 7/3 7:27a

MEREDITH: Some good friend called last night. Had to tell them about mommy. Guess I had a Danny Lapidus moment where I dump out everything on my mind out all at once. Love U. ... See you later   7/3 7:32a

LARRY: Maybe u should have been a doctor. Will be seen by an MS specialist

today. Arm still jerky. Only got
thiamine. Need spinal tap confirmation
before giving steroids. Going to try by
hand first. Problem with fluoroscope
maybe after weekend. Don't want to
wait 3 days for confirmation before
steroids can be given. Don't know if I
should make big fuss or just let them do
it by hand after lunch. What do you
think?   7/3 11:33a

> **MEREDITH:** Trying to call u.
> 7/3.11:33a

LARRY: Call me   7/3 11:33a

> **MEREDITH:** I think you have to
> have it done :(. I also think she was on
> Ativan the first time -- wasn't it after the
> MRI?   7/3 11:41a

LARRY: Idiot nurse just gave mommy
shot of Ativan w/o asking me.
Unbelievable.   7/3 12:45p

> **MEREDITH:** :(7/3 12:46p

> **MEREDITH:** Is she calm?
> 7/3 12:46

> **MEREDITH:** Maybe the nurse should
> give u one too?   7/3 12:47p

LARRY: She's knocked out...
7/3 12:47p

LARRY: Can't give pain pills because
too zonked. Should have given her

41

dilaudid pain IV followed by pill. It is
incredible how they drug people.
Mommy sleeping.   7/3 12:50p

                        MEREDITH: Oh no   7/3 12:54p

LARRY: Oh yes. Trying spinal tap
soon.   7/3 1:40p

LARRY: Tap complete. Mommy good!
7/3 2:31p

                        MEREDITH: That's great
                        7/3 3:03p

LARRY: With mommy. Jerky motion
now in leg kick. Spinal tap negative. 3 to
5 days of steroids started. Hopefully
mid-brain inflammation will subside.
7/4 7:44a

LARRY: More coherent ...Having
lovely sustained conversation with aide.
Steroids making mommy racy
7/4 10:10a

                        MEREDITH: Oh man :(
                        7/4 10:11a

                        MEREDITH: Did you get the pic of
                        Charlie and Dexter?   7/4 10:11a

LARRY: Send via email. Too small in
text format for mommy to see
7/4 10:13a

                        MEREDITH: Just sent.   7/4 7:20a

MEREDITH: Will come up around noon   7/4 7:21a

LARRY: K   7/4 7:21a

MEREDITH: Going to be there later. Need to take the train.   7/4 12:05p

LARRY: K brace yourself..some slurred speech added. Docs didn't come yet. 7/4 12:16p

MEREDITH: Ok waiting for Drew to get out of shower and will get dressed and come. I had a mild migraine but better now!   7/4 12:17p

LARRY: Later we need to shop for. PJ pants   7/4 2:24p

MEREDITH: Ok. Just got off train 7/4 2:32p

MEREDITH: At Bloomingdales. Got pjs -- everywhere near u is open but does not have them.   7/4 6:04p

LARRY: Good   7/4 7:10p

MEREDITH: Call me when you get up. Mommy Ativaned twice last night 7/5 5:47a

MEREDITH: What time are rounds - 9:30 or 10?   7/5 7:45a

MEREDITH: Cutting out again. On my way up   7/5 9:05a

43

LARRY: Take a look at these articles: Paraneoplastic Neurological Disorders - Central Nervous System (Brain and Spinal Cord): Paraneoplastic limbic encephalitis http://www.penncancer.org 7/5 9:27a

LARRY: Anti-NMDA receptor encephalitis – Take a look at Wikipedia http://en.m.wikipedia.org/wiki/Anti-NMDA_receptor_encephalitis 7/5 9:52a

MEREDITH: Morning. I'm up with the kids. How was the night? 7/6 7:04a

LARRY: K. She slept. Semi conscious now. Docs want feeding tube down her nose. Afraid chewed food might go to her lungs and cause respiratory problems.   7/6 8:46a

MEREDITH: On the phone Aunt Nina. She thought mommy was dead bc of the line in the email that said she is not the Sandy we know. But I explained to her that it was the chemicals etc. 7/6 9:08a

LARRY: Mommy lost her bridge. Lucky she didn't swallow it. 7/6 10:08a

LARRY: I'll take it home and put it in the same place as her ring and earrings . :-)   7/6 10:08a

MEREDITH: How is 1 or 1:30? I can come there and then maybe a late lunch? Or we can have lunch and then hospital? What works best for you? 7/6 10:37a

LARRY: Oh no. Did I see my last text? 7/6 10:39a

MEREDITH: Sounds good. Will call. 7/6 10:40a

MEREDITH: Running early. On train at 23rd. Will call when off   7/6 12:29p
MEREDITH: Walking down 96 th St... battery low   7/6 12:44p

LARRY: At hospital. Mommy agitated as I walked in. Given Ativan and now sleeping. Had nice and gentle conversation with Dr. Tao. CNS damage real possibility. Asked if I wanted to speak with Palliative Care. Will see social worker later. No immediate decision needed. Sam said my lymphoma theory is a possibility. Need conversations with Frankfurter, Kenneth and possibly an oncologist. Keep you updated. PS some typos in email I sent you earlier. If you find them, let me know. My spelling is worse than yours.   7/7 6:33a

MEREDITH: Saw your emails. Looks like we got the same amount of sleep. Leaving for the airport shortly. Will call when thru security and settled at gate. Love you.   7/7 6:39a

LARRY: Luv u 2   7/7 6:54a

LARRY: Kenneth off today. Spoke
with replacement. Wasted effort, but he
thinks he was comforting. Save me
from these drop by doctors who want
their fees. :-)   7/7 7:27a

> **MEREDITH:** Ug. You need the
> motion graphics app to blow them all
> up   7/7 7:29a

LARRY: Yes I do   7/7 7:29a

LARRY: Interesting conversation with
kidney doc. Lovely person. Says k
function down. Weekend team did most
check labs. Mommy not eating. Kidneys
may be damaged from dehydration over
weekend plus dye from MRI. Can come
back, but if not fed days to weeks. Dr
Faisel asked to put feeding tube in
through nose. Why didn't he ask when
mommy first stopped eating due to
sedation two days ago? Before I grant
permission, need discussion with
Frankfurter. Always come in here
expecting one thing and then they
throw the curve ball.   7/7 8:04a

> **MEREDITH:** Still with Frankfurter?
> 7/7 9:30a

LARRY: Conversation with F. He
wants a week to try plasmapheresis. Will
send palliative care and oncologist to
me. Good talk. Says there is a small

chance Mommy will recover but cannot promise CNS is not damaged. Have to wait and see. Read him the email I sent you. He gets it, but he still wants a week before throwing in the towel. Your reaction?   7/7 9:31a

LARRY: No documentation anywhere that treatment will work. Luv U
7/7 9:40a

LARRY: Thinking about nose feeding tube or IV feeding. Of the mind not to allow them to torture her any more. Let them wake Mommy and see if she is strong enough to swallow. She was Friday before they sedated her and forgot to feed her. Let natural course be complete rather than prolong life by artificial means. Thoughts?
On board?   7/7 11:12a

LARRY: Just spoke with Dr Fox, Torres' assistant surgeon. She gave me the oncology report over the phone Friday. Informed me Mommy's kidney is failing. More importantly helped me focus on bigger issue of what would mommy want.   7/7 11:29

LARRY: All the medical stuff, plasmapheresis, dialysis, radiation, feeding tube is not the point. Spoke with her for 25 minutes about our logic and how we were leaning not to prolong her life. She felt the process we went through was extremely thoughtful and she would be there to support any decision we made. She said mommy is very lucky to have two people who love her so much. She said she wished most people would have someone like us to love them the way we love mommy. Can't help the tears once I heard that. Still waiting on oncology and palliative care.   7/7 11:59a

LARRY: Met with Dr. David Erush, an oncologist. The good news is the plasmapheresis won't spread the cancer. The bad news is the steroids may already have done that. After long conversation Dr. Erush sees reasoned, sensitive logic in wanting mommy to have a quality of life which is reasonable.
If symptoms persist it is reasonable to assume Central Nervous System impairment. So that is the issue to stay focused on. Resident Faisel asked again about the nose feeder as if it was a solution. Afraid mommy won't make it without it. Dr. Erush feels food can come up from the tube and get into her lungs. Secondly, mommy is resting comfortably and is not feeling any hunger. Waiting on palliative care.
7/7 4:07

LARRY: Mommy just got flowers from Nina (unsigned but from San Diego). Also received a beautiful basket of flowers from Judy and Ed.
7/7 4:13p

MEREDITH: Just landed. [Note to reader: Meredith had a meeting at the Yahoo campus in California. I told her to go because Mommy would have wanted her to. She went reluctantly.]

LARRY: Nothing I read says anything positive so think i am in agreement with no feeding tubes :(.. Are you still leaning in that direction?   7/7 4:28p

MEREDITH: Yes!!!!   7/7 4:28p

LARRY: Ok....   7/7 4:29p

LARRY: Tonya, admin nurse is giving mommy a private room facing the park tonight.   7/7 4:29p

LARRY: Just spoke with Jay Frankfurter again. Wants to do plasmapheresis and then says you can go palliative care route. He is checking mommy's living will for loopholes :(Met with palliative care. They will consult with neurology, presumably to look for the large gaping loopholes in their brains. Will know tomorrow. Talk more seriously later tonight.
7/7 7:13p

[Note to reader: The living will was given to nurse on duty when Sandy first entered The Hospital Neurology Wing, but it was not put in electronic records the doctors use to evaluate and treat patients.]

> **MEREDITH:** Tell me if I should call back.   7/7 8:08p

LARRY: Why not?   7/7 9:27p

> **MEREDITH:** K good night. Luv U. 7/7 9:32p

LARRY: Me 2 iguana   7/7 9:33p

LARRY: With mommy. Neuro docs changed pain medicine to a small dose of Haldol. Didn't hold her for the night. Came in .. mommy in pain and was on and off for the night. Just awful. Got Frankfurter's resident, Tao who just came on to see her and get her a shot of Ativan. Exceptionally inept pain management. Spoke with Kenneth this morning. Frankfurter acceded to our request for palliative care and I should be meeting with their team this morning. Very sad but best thing for mommy. Love you   7/8 7:24a

LARRY: Ativan kicking in. Will meet with palliative pain people today so she never spends a other night like this one. Still groaning somewhat but she is calming down. Guess the plan was to raise mommy like Lazarus, with little pain meds to see if she could function. Ordered breakfast for her. Guess they wanted her to eat. Even got breakfast wrong. Mommy likes French Toast and bacon not mushy mystery eggs and a soggy English muffin. How stupid..... 7/8 8:28a

LARRY: Very nice one to one aide gently swabbing her mouth. Mommy calming down more. Good!
7/8 8:32a

LARRY: We made absolutely the right call with Mommy. Frankfurter concurs with our diagnosis that cancer had spread to lymph nodes resulting in paraneoplastic syndrome not abating and getting stronger. Palliative Team recommends you come home from California now.   7/8 10:23a

[Note to myself: How ironic Dr. Frankfurter came to me, after he met with the Palliative Care Team, to tell me Sandy is no longer a candidate for plasma washing - a procedure he so vehemently advocated the day before. Was it to make me feel better or was it to make him feel better? I guess I'll never know.]

                    MEREDITH: 1:20 flight out. Gets in at 10pm tonight   7/8 10:27a

LARRY: Good   7/8 10:30a

LARRY: Hospice 6 th floor
7/8 3:10a

                    MEREDITH: In the car with Drew. Headed to Mommy. On our way. Driving in.   7/8 11:27a
                    [Note to reader: Meredith and Drew made it to mommy's bedside after

midnight. She would die 2 days later at 6:26pm]

MEREDITH: Call when you get home. Charlie would like to talk to you. Though beware and remember she is 7 as she just said "is poppy going to marry someone else?" while decorating the grammy box.   7/9 7:36p

■

LARRY: At funeral home. Another service going on upstairs. Do you think I should crash and check out the competition? What's the worst that can happen?   7/14 11:10a

LARRY: Service steeped in religion. Escaped to Bagel Basket to have breakfast. On 90th and Amsterdam 7/14 11:23a

MEREDITH: K almost there 7/14 11:24a

LARRY: Thank you. I love you. Get some rest and talk tomorrow. 7/14 11:25a

3. The Emails

THE FOLLOWING EMAILS and Internet research are from June 14, 2014, to July 23, 2014. They illustrate the larger support system that was essential if Sandy, Meredith, and I were to survive this crisis. Meredith and I became gatekeepers because Sandy wanted her privacy. Yet, Sandy's family and friends were concerned, and Meredith and I felt an obligation to keep them informed.

There are a series of email blasts to friends and family about what we knew about Sandy's condition and when we knew it. Nothing is worse than not knowing, when you care for someone. Friends and family cared greatly, and we thought the best course of action was to be transparent.

Too often people choose to hide from an illness instead of confronting it. There are no right or wrong answers to what people choose to do when sorrow strikes. There are just hopes and fears, because in time sorrow will become part of everyone's life. The emails illustrate only a small sampling of the many emails sent and received during this period. They start with Sandy's going for a second opinion at The Hospital after her stroke and vestibular ear diagnosis at the Berkshires medical facility, and they lead up to a trip I took with Charlie to the Brooklyn Botanic Garden.

~

Subject: Response to the concerns of Indian Lake friends
Date: June 14, 2014

Hi Jeanette, Carl, Sherry and Lenny,

I know you are concerned and thank you for your calls, even if at times I don't have a chance to get back. On top of the vertigo (vestibular ear problem) she woke up yesterday with double vision. Spent day in The Hospital and it was determined it is not caused by another stroke (good news) or viral infection in the brain because of a clear spinal tap. Bad news is they don't yet know what is causing it. Appts with neurologist and ocular neurologist later in the week who hopefully can tell us what is going on. Trying to determine if ear and eye are related.

She is exhausted from the battery of tests and the anxiety of not knowing what is happening to her. I understand and share her feelings. She is home with me now and I look forward to tending to her this weekend before we start up with the doctors again next week. You can call and ask her how she is doing. Don't know what she will share, but she does care about you very much and your calls do make her feel better. Just please don't try to diagnose what is happening. Underneath her sort of upbeat tone, she is scared. Me too.

Maybe I will have better news next week.

Love,
Larry

Subject: Blast to friends – Sandy's Medical Condition
Date: June 19, 2014

Hi Guys,

Just too exhausted from the hospital to call each person back with the update I promised, but I did want you to know how important your support is to both Sandy and me. She is not ready to see anybody or even take phone calls at this point.

In simple terms, they found a mass above her aorta that they suspect is either an enlarged thymus gland or enlarged lymph nodes. Either condition can produce an autoimmune response, which inflames the nerves in the base of the brain. Doctor's hopeful either condition can be treated and the double vision, dizziness, etc. will stop. In either case it probably will be a hard three-month recovery period. If it is the thymus, it will be removed by surgery. If it is a lymphoma, it depends on the type of cell. In many cases New Chemo treatments work well. But we won't know anything until a biopsy is performed to see what the cells in the mass reveal and then it will take several days for radiologist/oncologist to read the cells. So I probably won't know anything definitive until Thursday of next week.

As of now these are the Doc's best guesses. They could do the biopsy and it could be something they didn't think of. I will keep you informed when we know what we are dealing with. It is ironic how quickly life can change. Hope for the best and again thank you for being there.

Larry

Subject: Blast to Friends – Sandy's Medical Update
Date: June 24, 2014 at 8:56 PM

Hi Everyone,

Promised I would share the news, since it is the least I can do for all the love and support you have been giving over the past several weeks. I can't tell you how much your flowers, emails and calls have done to keep the both of us sane. I think we are at the point where there is a light at the end of a tunnel. Not quite sure yet whether it is a light from heaven or hell. Sort of was hoping for a silver bullet but after all is said and done, there still are gray areas.

The biopsy final conclusion is a thymoma, which is a contained cancer in the thymus gland. This diagnosis is the best possible outcome from all the options we were considering. The Neurology Team is convinced of this diagnosis and when it is removed the double vision and lightheadedness will clear up in a couple of weeks. She will need some rehab for balance and walking. Short-term memory issues are caused by something else, maybe hospital stress, maybe not.

Dr. Torres, the thoracic surgeon, who is one of the best docs you can get and deals with this type of surgery personally, cannot assure me the double vision will dissipate when we remove the thymoma. He is unsure if it is causing the myasthenia gravis as the neurologists think. He wants some more tests and lab work back from the Mayo clinic to see if the MG diagnosis can be confirmed. He is correct in his approach, because if he cuts tomorrow he may have to go back in again for something else. He can't confirm that the long needle biopsy is correct until he operates.

We scheduled the removal of the Thymus gland on Friday. The good news is it is rare for this type of cancer to spread to the lymph nodes, and even if it did, it is caught early and the full CT scan from the neck to the pelvis shows no other indication of cancer. Hopefully Sandy and I will have a good quality of life for years to come.

Will continue to keep you informed on Sandy's progress. I can't put my feeling for each and every one of you into words. All I can say is thank you for getting both Sandy and me through the most trying time in our lives.

Love,
Larry

~

Subject: Blast – Update on Sandy
Date: June 27, 2014 at 2:23 PM
From: Meredith

Good news. Sandy had a successful surgery. Thymoma removed. Surgeon feels many symptoms will reverse in the next few weeks. Dad and I are very happy and thank you for all of your support.

~

A Note to the Reader
After the cancer surgery, Meredith and I hoped Sandy would become stronger and we could take her home and help her

heal. Slowly our hopes were shattered as the symptoms of paraneoplastic syndrome (PNS) continued to spread into Sandy's nervous system. It was no longer only her double vision and dizziness. She developed an uncontrollable movement, which jerked her arm.

Her personality changed where she had to react to every stimulus in the room. She could hardly walk or get out of bed. In some lucid moments she told me she was in trouble. Further down the line she told me she was lost. Sandy, who was one of the most peaceful, centered personalities ever, became crazed, trying to rip out the various intravenous leads attached to her. Her personality had changed, but Meredith and I kept hoping she would return to the Sandy we knew.

In seeking answers, both Meredith and I decided to learn everything we could about Sandy's condition and the quality of life she would experience. While the neurologists at The Hospital told me the condition was "treatable," the question became: With what outcomes? Even with the inept pain management from June 30th until now, the Palliative Care option was never suggested by any of the specialists, which is a curious symptom the hospital should diagnose.

Palliative Care first intervened the evening of July 7th. Once involved, they were remarkable in seeing the whole patient, her needs, and her wishes. It was later explained that The Hospital is known to have a model where the patient is treated by both the Palliative Care Team and the interventional specialists working in tandem. I wish Sandy could have experienced this model much earlier, for it would have avoided much of the pain she suffered and her family suffered when forced to make decisions on Sandy's treatment.

~

Subject: Blast – Update on Sandy's Medical Condition
Date: July 5, 2014 at 1:58 PM

It's Meredith (writing for Larry). The doctor's latest diagnosis is limbic encephalopathy, which is part of a paraneoplastic syndrome caused by the thymoma. They suspect the obstructing protein is an NMDA receptor in the antibodies. She is undergoing 3-5 days of steroid therapy, which if successful will be followed by 12 days of a plasma washing to try to rid her of any chemical causing her condition. At this point, the stuff is masking the Sandy we know and the doctors are keeping her sedated to move forward with the therapies. This is all very rare and devastating and they feel this is the best shot that we have for her to recover. We will be in touch when we have new information. Thank you for all of the support.

Meredith

~

A Note to the Reader
From the Mayo Clinic's website I learned that, while the cancer itself may be curable, it is the paraneoplastic syndrome that can "result in substantial morbidity." It may cause "irreversible pathological changes to the nervous system." In an abstract from *Clinical Neurology and Neurosurgery* (Vol. 107, Issue 2, Feb 2005), I learned that few reports deal with the quality-of-life concerns and that in many cases palliative care was all that could be offered. "Memory impairment is often irreversible."

Neurologists say that by the time PNS is diagnosed, there is substantial damage to the central nervous system. What is worse is that experimental treatments the doctors were advocating, like corticosteroids and plasmapheresis, have "generally been unsuccessful." The prognosis is that even when the tumor is cured, the majority of patients stabilize and "remain severely disabled for the rest of their lives."

~

Subject: A Hard Day
Date: July 6, 2014 at 5:00 PM

Dear Friends,

Today was an awfully hard day at the hospital. I had asked for consultations with various doctors to try and figure out the best course of action for Sandy's treatment. I had individual meetings with Sandy's neurologist, several of his residents, a thoracic surgeon, an oncologist, and a pain management team.

To get the most out of such meetings, I have learned to do my research. At night, I really don't sleep all that much, which I suspect the more alert of you have managed to figure out by now. I really went back and studied the scientific literature on Sandy's rare syndrome, everywhere from the Mayo Clinic, The Dana Foundation, the NIH, The University of Pennsylvania, etc.

This way I was sure I could ask focused questions that needed to be asked. (Ironically and independently, I later found out Meredith was going through the same night research process at her house.) I would say each meeting, as the doctors popped into Sandy's room between 6 in the morning to 6 in the evening, lasted a good 25 minutes. They were sustained discussions, not without some tears, with some very bright and caring people. I won't share them with you now because the amount of information would go on forever and I know my processing system: I need a few days to make sense out of all that was said. I left the hospital zonked from the day and the lack of sleep.

When I came home, Sammy handed me the mail, as he always does, and a shopping bag. Up in the apartment, I open the gift, because I thought that after this day I needed the liquor first. It was a bottle of a gin, made in Brooklyn, that Barbara and Lou knew I particularly liked.

Then I opened the card and was completely blown away by the sentiments within. It is good to have caring friends in our life who are supportive in critical times. It made a hard day much better. I promise to use the Yura gift certificates and will put them in the same safe place as Sandy's diamond ring and earrings. :-)

You guys are the best,
Larry

P.S. Barbara, since I recognized your Catholic school penmanship on the card, would you be kind enough to mail me Debby and Tom's email? I do not have them on my home computer and would like to forward this note to them.

~

Subject: Update – Sandy's Medical Condition
Date: July 7, 2014

Hi All,
I transferred Sandy into the Hospice. Dying is part of life and I felt it was my responsibility to give the love of my life a good, dignified, painless death. She was so ravaged by a disease with no real chance of a cure that it was unacceptable for her to continue treatments, as some doctors wished. She never wanted to live a low quality of life where basic functions of walking, memory, eyesight and muscle movement could be part of a never-ending rehabilitation program plagued with likely relapses of paraneoplastic syndrome. I am thankful this disease only lasted a month and it will not be a prolonged death. She needs relief and peace. It was the hardest decision Meredith and I ever had to make, but we did what Sandy wanted. If there are any of you who do not have living wills, I suggest that you make them as soon as possible. Some doctors tend to think with their heads, not their hearts.

She still is not accepting visitors at the hospice and I will be spending the next several days or weeks with her. It is unclear when the end will come. My hope is it will be soon. Please understand I won't have the energy to return emails or phone calls for a few days, but I will let you know where and when services will be held for those of you in the city who wish to attend. If I have left anyone off the list who knows Sandy and should be informed, I would consider it a favor if you did so.

With Love,
Larry

P.S. Please forgive me if a few of you are hearing this news for the first time. It has been an exhausting month and I just have not had the energy to call everyone.

~

A Note to the Reader
The writer of the next email, daughter-in-law of dear friends of Sandy and me, sent this message before knowing the full extent of Sandy's condition at the time.

Subject: Stepping into your circle
Date: July 8, 2014
From: Jill London

Hi, Larry. It's Jill London. Adam has kept me in the loop from the beginning, but as this is such a private experience for you, Sandy, and Meredith, I have kept in the shadows. I hope it's ok that I am stepping into your circle momentarily to tell you that my thoughts and prayers are with you all. I don't know the specifics of Sandy's current prognosis, but I do know that your world has become a surreal, scary place and I am so sad for that. I imagine the only absolute is that there is no certainty at all. Remember that the unknown is partnered with hope. As long as there is a window, no matter how small, sunshine and the promise of a brighter day may enter.

I think about you and Sandy all the time. I pray that although your lives may never be the same, they will still be filled with love, joy, and the promise of laughter and new adventures. In the meantime, during these long tough days in the hospital, try to leave your glass half full :) I know that there are many people in the wings just waiting for your cue to rush to you and Sandy's bedside. Everyone is prepared and longing to support and embrace you both as is! If there is anything I can do to help, distract, support ... Please do not hesitate to call on me. The girls are in camp so I have my days open and I'm only a hop-skip from Manhattan. Miracles do happen.

Love,
Jill

~

Subject: Boonins are devastated
Date: July 8, 2014
From: Fran and Bob Boonin

Dearest Larry,

Words can never express the depth of the feelings that have engulfed us. We are truly devastated! To lose Sandy is unfathomable! We know we are not alone in our feelings. Those who know her can't get over what a truly exceptional person she is, in every way. It is hard to believe that such a beautiful (inside and out), vibrant, intelligent, active and wonderful person could be ravaged by such an unmerciful illness so quickly. Somehow, denying the reality of her condition allowed us to believe that she would overcome it.

Last night we, along with Libby and Steve and Jeannette and Carl, toasted to her recovery, only to come home to your beautifully written but gut-wrenching email. You, Meredith and Sandy are incredibly brave! Your love and devotion, and the

love from those around you, will get you through this. We will
talk when you are able.

With much love,
Fran and Bob

~

Subject: The Last Update [from Meredith]
Date: July 10, 2014

Sandy died at 6:26pm. She was surrounded by my dad, my
husband Drew and me at her passing. The family takes solace
in the fact that we did everything we could for her. Funeral
arrangements are being made and we will inform you of the
specifics by tomorrow afternoon. Although it is devastating we
are thankful that she is at peace.

~

Subject: Condolences from Bria, age 12, and Cienna, age 7
(Jill and Adam London's Children)
Date: July 16, 2014

Dear Larry,

I am so sorry to hear about Sandy. She was a lovely, nice lady who was very lucky to have you as a husband!

To continue the cookie legacy of our friendship, we have enclosed a batch of homemade cranberry pecan white chocolate chip cookies! Bon appetite! And feel free to send back any critiques you have! ☺

I can't wait to see you again soon! Enjoy the cookies!

Love,

Bria

~

Subject: Cookies to the Max
Date: July 17, 2014

Hi Bria and Cienna,

Know what happened today? Opened up a cardboard box and there were cookies. Now, I am on a low carb diet, but these cookies look so good that I am going to eat them all up. Who taught you how to make such delicious cookies? These were special cookies. When I saw them and read both your notes, I cried a little. But they weren't sad tears. They were happy tears that you baked these special cookies for me. One of the immutable rules of life is that you never critique happy cookies. And not only do the cookies make me happy, the floating plastic boat you sent them in will be great when I take a bath. I can pretend I am a sea captain delivering my cargo of cookies to a safe port near my big toe. I won't put all the cookies in the boat because it may sink in the tub and nobody wants soggy, bathwater cookies. I'll put just enough in to make sure they stay crisp and dry.

Thank you for your special cookies and your thoughts about Sandy. Like your cookies, she was sort of special too. Will both of you give your parents a big hug from me? Hope to see you guys in Becket soon.

Your friend,
Larry

~

The Institutions

THE FOLLOWING EMAILS deal with two commercial institutions and how they reacted to Meredith and me right after Sandy's passing. One is Too Big To Fail Bank (TBTF), where Sandy and I had a safe deposit box. The other is Papyrus, an upscale paper store that sells stationery, including recognition notes for people attending funerals. Their contrasting corporate cultures speak volumes regarding how people should be treated after a loss.

The story starts with a letter I wrote to a regional manager at TBTF, railing against the treatment that Meredith and I experienced when we tried to get Sandy's will from the safe deposit box. We were denied access because TBTF bankers must follow the requirements of New York State Law when a joint owner of a box has died.

But while the bankers clearly know how to toe the mark when it comes to locking customers out of safe deposit boxes, they seem to be a bit less "compliant" about money laundering, financial trading manipulation, and violating sanctions against Iran. The emails show the morass of bureaucratic detail people can experience when a spouse dies.

Luckily, I had developed a good friendship with Thomas Schalk, my Merrill Financial Advisor, and, of course, John Ciarelli, my lawyer, who helped me through the maze. I wanted to undertake a quest with TBTF to get them to realize the way they treat people could benefit from understanding how The Hospice treats people. Some would describe such a quest as pissing into the wind, but nonetheless, my advisors helped me focus on what was needed.

~

Subject: Leaving TBTF as a Premier Customer After 10 Years
To: Bill Wiseman
Date: July 16, 2014 at 9:49 PM

Dear Mr. Wiseman,

I think that you, as regional manager and David Arabelly's supervisor, may want to take a closer look at some of the practices at his bank. I refer to a specific interaction with Chris Warmth and David Arabelly for which I hear many apologies which no longer cut it with me. The result is not only am I seriously considering moving substantial assets out of your bank, but telling you that you had a shot at another major investment from my wife's life insurance policy. After my experience today, I doubt very much it is going to happen.

Too bad for you, but I need a bank where a relationship manager and vice president understand what a relationship is. My daughter and I did not feel that today. Here is the scenario:

1. Spoke with Mr. Warmth yesterday about opening up a joint account with my daughter. He told me he wasn't sure if I could access bill pay on my current internet account because my wife is the primary, but he wasn't sure, and I was to have a 9:00 AM meeting with Reagan, a Premier Customer Rep in Buffalo. (I later found out his assumption of me not being able to access the bill pay feature was incorrect.)
2. Waited next morning at 9:00 AM. No call. Waited till 9:15, no call. Called Morris Birch, my previous relationship manager, who I found competent. Emailed Reagan, but she was going into a meeting. She had the appointment for tomorrow.

3. Went to my 2:00 PM with Mr. Warmth. He was having lunch and arrived 15 minutes late. I, on the other hand, skipped my lunch to be there on time, as did my daughter. This is the first

time I met my new relationship manager. Told him about today's meeting being scheduled for tomorrow. Told him he promised me an email printout of all the incoming and outgoing bill pay activity, and that didn't happen either. He said he was stretched thin because he was covering two banks and he was sorry. I hate meaningless apologies. He said he scheduled the meeting for tomorrow with Reagan, but forgot to inform me. Now here is a guy you can trust with your investment portfolio.

4. In the meantime, my daughter, who is on the safe deposit card, tries to go to the box. She is rudely stopped by a woman downstairs and then told by the bank manager that she is not on the account. Turns out of course she is on the account but they did not read the card correctly.

5. Then told will have to get an intestate letter because I told them my wife is dead, and I am going to pilfer the vast fortune in the box. At this point, I see all the stupidity of the hospital system right in your little branch on my corner. I hear about New York State law, we could lose our jobs, but not one word of condolence for my hypothetically dead wife who you feel is actually dead. If she is dead, why aren't your people more compassionate? In fact, Mr. Warmth glared at me and said, "Are you refusing to get an intestate letter?" I decided then not to open up a joint account with my daughter as I had planned. Mr. Warmth did call Reagan and supposedly got me access to the online bill pay feature of your internet banking.

My daughter too, who with me experienced the most horrendous 40 days of our lives, was taken aback by how mechanical your employees are. A little grace and a little charm could have defused the situation. I will get a lawyer to get a court order to open up the box to get our wills, etc. By the way, Reagan is competent, and I will keep my meeting with her tomorrow.

6. The branch manager, as I apprised him of the situation, could only say, "I apologize," again and again. Be assured, I am not interested in apologies. I am interested in my accounts being managed competently and my relationships to have some sense of compassion, which was sorely lacking at this branch.

I can accept New York State law. What I can't accept is a lack of feeling from your employees. You are the supervisor. Change things.

I don't know what you can do to earn my trust at this point. You need to change my relationship manager immediately. I need to deal with someone with more clout and competence. I don't want to be treated rudely, nor does my daughter. Please call me if you have any questions; after all, I have been a premier customer for ten years or so. As a result of today's incident, I think I will start to shop around for places that can do well with my financial assets and cash flow. When a bank feels a customer is unimportant, especially in a time of personal crisis, it is an indication it is time to move on. Would you not agree?

Sincerely,
Lawrence Abrams

~

Subject: Fwd: Dana and Linda vs leaving TBTF Premier after 10 or so years
To: Bill Wiseman
Date: July 17, 2014 at 7:35:02 AM

Dear Mr. Wiseman,

As a follow-up to yesterday's email, I tried to log on to TBTF internet banking, following the precise protocol given to me by my relationship manager yesterday. Log on rejected. Customer Service representative and Bank Manager didn't suggest at the time to check success of log in using my iPhone when my daughter and I were at the bank to ensure that what was communicated to us would work. Mr. Arabelly did say, "If there's anything else we can do for you, please let me know."

Again, he and my relationship manager failed to grasp what follow-through I needed to make the situation better. Will follow up by myself when Reagan calls me this morning. Hope she calls as scheduled. I was not given her phone # or email. Ironically, below is a note that I sent on the same day to the regional manager of Papyrus. Read it. At Papyrus I experienced sensitivity, and at TBTF I experienced insensitivity. When read together, the letters form a case study as to why these two enterprises, which exist to sell paper to consumers and businesses, are so different. Which email would you prefer to receive?

So the management question is why didn't you receive it? Would request you forward me the email of your superior as well as the C.E.O. for TBTF Bank USA, so I may forward my two emails to them. I am sure you will agree they form an interesting case study in business management.

Sincerely,
Lawrence Abrams

Begin forwarded message:

Subject: Dana (96th) and Linda (69th)
To: Massiel Pena, supervisor Papyrus
Date: July 16, 2014 at 1:09 PM

Hi Massiel,

I am a Papyrus customer who is writing to inform you that two of your salespersons exhibited remarkable sensitivity to me when my wife was ill in The Hospital and when she eventually died from an extremely rare illness, and I needed appreciation notes for people who attended the service.

Dana, when I stopped in to see if certain paper could be used to block out an eyeglass lens to stop my wife's double vision, could not have been sweeter. There was nothing in the store that worked well, but another customer had a thick shopping bag and Dana helped me cut the lens cover from a template I had.

After my wife died, I knew I couldn't use the funeral home cards, so I remembered Dana's kindness and gave her a call. We spoke about what I needed and she referred me to Linda at your 69th street store, who in turn was exceptionally kind and helpful in selecting the right card, which she had to import from the Grand Central Station store. She worked on the layout with me and cared that it was done well.

I suspect that, as a manager, you often have to deal with customers who complain. Here, I am bringing to your attention two of your employees who went above and beyond to help me during a critical period. Please recognize their efforts for me.

Sincerely,
Lawrence Abrams

~

From: Lawrence Abrams
Date: July 19, 2014 8:20 AM
To: Sarah Dinzy, Art Therapist, The Hospice
Subject: Opening communications

Hi Sarah,

Need your help on an idea that might be able to put the Palliative Care professionals at The Hospital in touch with the Office of Corporate Giving at TBTF Bank USA. If they do listen to my approach letter, who would be a good point person on your team for them to contact? Please provide me with the contact information.

In a nutshell, my local TBTF bank was just awful in dealing with my financial requests. They had zero to less than zero sensitivity to what my daughter and I were experiencing after

Sandy's death. Instead of assisting us through a process they threw up frustrating road blocks. I'll spare you the specifics, but I did document the incident to a regional manager, Bill Wiseman. I'll send you the second letter I wrote, comparing TBTF and Papyrus, so you can see my thinking. He is calling me this morning. I am sure he'll apologize, but I find those type of apologies unfulfilling. Change the behavior of your staff and a corporate culture that allows staff members to act the way they did.

To do this I decided I would forward a letter to the president of TBTF USA suggesting a win-win solution, where TBTF gets its Corporate Giving head to meet with the Palliative Care Team to find out if there are any needs they can support. In turn, TBTF would see how to deal with families in grief and sensitize their staff, so what happened to my daughter and me won't be repeated. They can get some much needed positive publicity after their drug-laundering scandal.

It is a long shot, but I think I can convince this regional manager to get on board. Whether I am successful or not, this effort is helping me heal so I have nothing to lose and everything to gain. Thanks again to you and the team that provided the much needed support to Sandy, me, and my family.

Best,
Larry Abrams

~

From: Sarah Dinzy, Art Therapist, The Hospice
Date: Jul 21, 2014, at 5:41 PM
Subject: Re: Opening communications
To: Lawrence Abrma

Hi Larry,
Thanks so much for reaching out and for sharing this story.
I am so sorry to hear that you experienced such little
sensitivity during what I assume is one of the most sensitive
times in your life. I am happy to hear that your efforts with
TBTF are helping you heal.

I am happy to connect you to Hattie Eden, she works in the
Palliative Care office as the administrative manager. She is
wonderful. I have copied her to this email so feel free to
reach out to her directly. Wishing you and your family well....

Best wishes,
Sarah

Sarah Dinzy, MA, LCAT, ATR-BC, CCLS
Board Certified Child Life Art Therapist
Pediatrics and Palliative Care

~

Subject: Re: Opening communications
Date: July 21, 2014 at 6:47 PM
To: Sarah Dinzy, Art Therapist, The Hospice

Hi Sarah,

Don't know how to reach Hattie Eden directly because I don't see an email. Please forward this brief note to her. Reached out to a Bill Wiseman, who is a regional manager, about soliciting the corporate giving office to have a conversation with The Hospice's Palliative Care Unit to see how to deal with bereavement issues. Said he would kick my idea up the corporate ladder, but couldn't make promises. He said he will get back to me by the end of the week. Said I don't care if they donate $50 or $50,000 to your unit, I think TBTF's corporate structure has to be more like what I experienced at the hospice and at Papyrus. If he shows any interest and can rally the corporate giving people I will let Hattie know.

Best,
Larry Abrams

~

From: Eden, Hattie
Subject: RE: Opening communications
Date: July 22, 2014 at 12:47:12 PM EDT
To: Lawrence Abrams
Cc: Meredith Jacoby , Dinzy, Sarah

Good afternoon Mr. Abrams,

I am so sorry to hear of the ordeal you are going through and so grateful that during such a difficult time, you are thinking of us. It truly is through the kindness of folks like you that our unit has been allowed to help so many patients and families. We appreciate your support more than I could adequately express, so let me just say: thank you, thank you, thank you!!

Please do not hesitate to contact me or pass along my contact information if you think I can be of any assistance. Many, many thanks again,

Hattie
Hattie Eden, Administrative Manager

~

From: Lawrence Abrams
Subject: Re: Opening communications
Date: July 25, 2014 at 3:37:32 PM
To: Hattie Eden, Bill Wiseman

Hi Hattie,

Just got off the phone with Bill Wiseman, Regional Manager for TBTF bank US, and he has approached the Corporate Giving Office. He said they were prepared to make a donation in my wife's name. I have no idea what the specifics are, but I told him I would give him your contact information and you could work out the details with him or his designee at Corporate Giving.

I feel much better about the corporate structure of TBTF wanting to help the place which treated Sandy with comfort and dignity. Please thank your wonderful staff, including Zena and Sarah. Zena, as always, hugged me and spent time listening when I unexpectedly dropped by to find a grief counselor. My grandchild, Charlie, acting on Sarah's suggestion, is still using the memory box every Sunday as a constructive way to process

78

her grief. Your Palliative Team of doctors advocated for my wife, on my behalf, and I simply cannot thank them enough. Please let me know the outcome of your conversation with TBTF.

Thanks,
Lawrence (Larry) Abrams

~

From: "Eden, Hattie"
Subject: RE: Opening communications
Date: July 25, 2014 at 3:52:05 PM EDT
To: Lawrence Abrams, Bill Wiseman

Good afternoon Mr. Abrams,

I'm very glad to hear that TBTF will be reaching out to me with a donation in your wife's memory, but even more glad to hear that you've been granted some resolve in this situation. I cannot express enough how rewarding it is for every member of our team to have support and appreciation of families like you! Thank you for everything!! I will certainly pass along your comments and will let you know as soon as I hear from TBTF. Have a lovely weekend!

Best,
Hattie

~

A Note to the Reader
In the end, TBTF donated $100 to the The Hospice. It was not from the Corporate Giving Department. I am not quite sure

what percentage of their corporate profits that is. It became obvious to me that TBTF corporate culture had no interest in meeting with the hospice staff. I decided to move my money to another bank. Ciao, TBTF; we are done. In contrast., the following email from Ellyn Toscano, Phil Tama's second wife, a lawyer who presently runs New York University's Campus in Florence, Italy, among others, wrote an email that simply staggered me with its sensitivity and comprehension.

~

Subject: Re: Reaching Out
To: Lawrence Abrams
Date: July 20, 2014 at 5:18 PM
From: Ellyn M. Toscano

Larry,

We should definitely meet up in August. I know you cannot imagine feeling relief from the pain you feel now – it is unimaginable that it could get better. In a way, we always feel like it is disloyal to feel relief, and so we invest in the loss. But somebody wise said to me that the pain from a loss this great never abates – even now when I think of my first husband's death, so many years ago, it is as if he died yesterday.

But – and this is the good news – the time between the memories, the episodes of pain, extends with time and you find the time and space to live free of pain. Again, I do not believe that you could possibly understand what I mean since you will have to experience it yourself. But when people say to you that it gets better with time, and you resent them for saying so because you don't want to feel better with time, they're right.

About Italy. Though it is too soon, you do need to think about a future, and plan for it and give yourself some relief. The first Christmas after my husband's death, the thought of being in NY with the Christmas lights and spirit that I so loved while he was alive caused me *terror*. I booked a trip to Hawaii, the place I thought would least resemble my conception of Christmas. I went alone, for two weeks. It was the best, most therapeutic thing I could do because I learned I could survive alone, without him.

In short, give yourself some time. There are no rules, correct ways to feel or act. Don't try to meet anybody else's expectations. Just let it happen, as it must. And let all of us help, if we can. I am sure this is more than you want. I know that you lived with your wife with great joy, that you brought her joy and comfort, and you will have to keep that in mind while you grieve. Stay close to your daughter, and her children, and let them help you.

Ellyn

~

A Note to the Reader
In trying to recover, I found my grandchildren to be the best therapy. After Sandy's death, I was worried how I would react given the circumstances. In the following email to Meredith, I report on my findings. (My nickname for her is Moosey.)

Subject: A day with Charlie
To: Meredith Jacoby

Date: July 23, 2014

Hi Moosey,

Really lovely day with Charlie at Botanical Gardens. Got t-shirts for Charlie and Dexter, so I will have a prompt to remember the day when I see them wearing the presents. Charlie wanted Dexter to have a sort of similar color to hers. She picked medium green for herself and light green for him.

Really talked about all sorts of things but very little about Grammy which was fine. I did tell Charlie that if she had any questions she wanted to ask me she could. She hugged me gently and went on talking about her day at performing arts camp, singing her songs she needs for Friday's performance.

On the way home she discovered a golf ball from a driving range in the back of my car. She asked me could she keep it. I said yes. Later, when we were in your front yard, she told me she wanted to put it in her grammy box because grammy was a good golfer. She told me Sunday was her day to put her memories in the box. I told her grammy and I were just starting to play golf and we really weren't good yet.

"But," I said, "Grammy always liked learning something new and golf was something new." Charlie thought about this for a while and then told me, "Grammy does like learning something new. Maybe she is learning to read the dirt that she is in." She said it not in a distressed way, but a wonderful way which helped her visualize Grammy's essence. I just said, "Maybe you're right," and we went on to looking at a ladybug.

Grammy always marveled at her mind. She is some child.
Dexter too was sweet as can be with me. I got hugs and kisses
from him.

Love,
Daddy

4. The Funeral

At 2 PM on Monday, July 14th, at Plaza Jewish Community Chapel, Sandy's service commenced. Meredith and I hadn't known what to expect in terms of numbers, but the Chapel, which holds about 200 people, was packed. We did know what we wanted the service to be. My daughter, who is a Yahoo executive responsible for an events planning team in New York, threw herself into planning the goodbye event. We both knew we did not want anyone who hadn't known Sandy to talk about her. We knew a religious officiant could be objective and engage us in the rituals. We wanted people to speak who were subjective and could explain Sandy at different parts of her life. My promise to my wife when she lay dying in front of me – to share her legacy with her grandchildren when they were old enough to understand who she was – had to be our central focus.

Meredith and I explained our concept to Barbara Weinstein, a good friend and neighbor of mine in both Manhattan and Becket. She had experienced loss in her own life, knew us well, understood Sandy's ordeal, and had the right organizational skills, coupled with a sense of humor. She was the perfect choice. At one point, through the flurry of emails and spreadsheets needed to realize the event, she wrote that she wanted her next job to be Meredith's assistant. Barbara graciously accepted our proposal to be our officiant. She handled her role with such sensitivity and competence that at the end of the service, one of our friends propositioned her for his funeral. At least, I think it was for his funeral.

A cohort of friends were asked to reflect individually on various periods of Sandy's life. In such a format, people who knew only a section or two of Sandy's life would be able to understand the full picture.

One person in the audience said to me after the service, "My God, are all your friends that articulate?" I answered, "Not usually." But I knew they were. They thought about Sandy in their lives, and distilled her essence with a variety of anecdotes. They gave me the gift of their words to share with my grandchildren, which is the best gift anyone ever gave me. Their remarks follow.

~

BARBARA WEINSTEIN is a professor and a founding executive officer of the audiology and health sciences doctoral programs at The City University of New York's Graduate Center. She and her husband, Lou, were Sandy's neighbors in Manhattan and in Indian Lake in the Berkshires.

I am a friend of Larry and Sandy from the Berkshires and New York. We live in the same apartment building. We volunteered for the Clinton Global Initiative, and I was honored to witness Sandy's being asked on many occasions to be a placeholder for Hillary Clinton, and if I remember correctly, Bill, as well.

Welcome and thank you all for coming to honor and remember our larger-than-life relative, friend, or colleague.

Sandy's wheels were always turning. She did everything with such grace, modesty, and exactitude, which was readily apparent, especially if you were her opponent in tennis or bridge. She had no pretenses, despite her many gifts. She had a prodigious memory but never held a grudge. The daughter of Holocaust survivors, her roots and the family into which she was born were the foundation of who she was. Early on, Sandy learned what really mattered in life. Her humble beginnings were the rudder that steadied and steered her toward a future filled with accomplishment, a love of life, travel, languages, and a desire to constantly take on new challenges. In private, she and Larry were so grateful and marveled at their life and the sensitive and accomplished daughter they raised. Of course, Charlie and Dexter were the icing on the wonderful life she and Larry built and shared.

Untethered from where it all began for her, remembering her origins – these are the keys that opened the door to her future as an educator's educator. To me, her approach to life, their love affair, and her recognition that immortality and eternal life are not ours to have, were the greatest lesson plans she ever wrote and lived.

Few lives are fulfilled; there is always more to be done. Knowing the inevitability of death, Sandy had the unique human quality of living life better. A purposeful life is contingent on attentiveness to our mortality. Knowing Sandy, as I believe I do, the very knowledge that our days are numbered informed her philosophy of making each day count. Sandy had so much more life to live, but make no doubt about it, she is the gift that will keep on giving. Death cannot rob Sandy from us; memories confer mortality. As John Greenleaf Whittier observed, "Grant but memory to us, and we can lose nothing by death." Sandy, we weep for you and grieve because you touched our lives with beauty and simplicity. We are all in agreement. You were good to life.

Enough from me. Now you will hear from Sandy's friends, relatives, and colleagues about the ardor with which Sandy approached life and her love of it. Sandy's immortality lives on in the many lives she touched, as will become immediately apparent. First and foremost, allow me to channel the love of Sandy's life, Larry, including his tears: "With deep gratitude I would like to thank all the people who have come to this service. The last 40 days were some of the most horrific days of our lives. But 40 days are short compared to the rich, full lifetime of happiness we had together. This service is designed to encapsulate her life with different speakers remembering Sandy in different phases of her life. Meredith and I wanted it that way, so her grandchildren, when they are truly old enough to discover who their grandmother was, will have her legacy before them. We thank our family who came from distant lands – Canada, Israel, and from across the border in New Jersey – for being here, as well as her many friends. Sandy, raised in a European immigrant tradition, was modest and would not want all of this attention. In saying goodbye, my love, you deserve no less."

~

JOHN CIARELLI, of Ciarelli and Dempsey, is a practicing attorney in Riverhead, Long Island. He and his wife, Carolyn, met Sandy in college and remained friends ever since then. They reside in St. James, Long Island.

The Years 1964 to 1971

This is a tribute to a woman with whom my wife, Carolyn, and I have been friends for almost 50 years. I am here to talk about the early years of that friendship, and believe me, remembering that far back is a challenge. If the somewhat disjointed memories of those college years do not clearly express the overriding theme of these comments, this is it: That Sandy's character was as put together then as it was throughout the years. The traits of that character we had the good fortune to know and love – intelligence, honesty, love of culture; the list goes on and I am sure others will speak of them – were there 50 years ago and throughout our relationship.

Of necessity, some of these recollections include my friend Larry, Carolyn, and me, but it is not about us. Carolyn helped me with this, and to the extent that our memory is a little hazy, well, none of you were there and there is no way Larry remembers.

Larry and I met in September 1964. We were assigned to the same floor in a residence hall at SUNY Stony Brook. There were about 30 of us strangers thrust together and, for the most part, we bonded quickly and traveled as a pack. It quickly became apparent that, unlike most of the rest of us,

Larry exhibited an unusual degree of serenity for a college freshman. We soon learned that his serenity was called Sandy Hoffman. She was from Brooklyn, and she was his girlfriend. It was a while before we got to meet her. Typically, Larry left the campus at 4pm on Friday in his maroon Buick four-door and returned late on Sunday night.

As time went on, little tidbits about Sandy Hoffman would be revealed. She goes to Brooklyn College, lives at home, going to be a teacher, good at languages. After a while we got to the important stuff – nice body, tall-thin-sexy, great personality. I am not suggesting that Larry was explicit in his descriptions, but we saw a picture and the rest was communicated in other ways, including, but not limited to, the rush to the Buick on Friday afternoons.

It was not until the spring semester of freshman year that Sandy made her first live personal appearance at Stony Brook. All of our (the pack's) expectations were met. She was lovely, sophisticated, friendly, centered (a concept that would not be invented for another 20 years or so), and she liked/loved Larry. We had no way of knowing whether the word had been spoken at that time, although she acted towards him as if it had been. She stayed in a girls dorm with some Brooklyn friends. For our part (the pack's, that is) we registered our approval to Larry in the form of various noises and facial expressions.

Humans mated, figuratively speaking, early in those days. Carolyn and I met during the blackout of 1965. As time went on, our couples' social circle was formed. The first event that the four of us attended as couples was the "Spring Fling."

Sandy would come out to Stony Brook anytime we could conjure a sufficient excuse. We all enjoyed these events. It was fun and relaxing to be together. The frequency of our contact did not matter, not then and not in recent years. We were friends. You knew with Sandy that if she was your friend, your friendship would endure. We were coming of age together

Then there was the summer of 1967. Sandy overcame some resistance from her parents, escaped from Brooklyn, and we – Larry, Sandy, Carolyn, Mike, Roni, Cliff, and I – shared two off-campus garden apartments that were leased by the university.

The boys stayed in one apartment and the girls in another – a laughable arrangement by today's standards. Sandy got a summer job in a dental office nearby, Larry did his student teaching, Carolyn and I worked at the university. It was a great summer. Sandy loved it.

Over the years we often talked about the stories and personalities of that summer. Carolyn and I got to know Sandy very well. She was smart and focused; she freely expressed her opinions and was proud of her heritage. She was then the same person you knew and loved throughout the years.

The next year went pretty fast and, we assumed, Sandy planned the wedding for the end of June 1968. Sandy's good taste and sophistication were reaffirmed by her striking wedding dress in contrast to Larry's Nehru jacket. Being a little ahead of the curve maturity-wise, she honed what has become her self-evident decorating skill on their first apartment. To my knowledge, Sandy and Larry were the first newlyweds in the New York metropolitan area to have Country French furniture.

Many of you know that among Sandy's many talents was a facility for languages. Carolyn and I made arrangements to meet Sandy and Larry on the French Riviera in August 1971. We did not know it at the time, but Meredith was there, too. It was a day or so after Nixon had devalued the dollar. It was the weekend, we had driven from Italy and had no francs; no one was accepting our traveler's checks. Nothing is better than traveling in a foreign country with a friend that speaks the language. Sandy, as always – centered, capable, in control – solved the problem.

In reflecting on those years and the past almost 50 years, I was struck by the depth and consistency of her spirit and the friendship that we shared throughout the years. That we remember clearly.

With love,
Carolyn & John Ciarelli

~

WILLIAM SIGELAKIS and VERONICA BOYHAN: William Sigelakis was the principal of John Dewey High School in Brooklyn and, later, of Herricks High School on Long Island. He and his wife, Lori, lived in an adjacent neighborhood in Brooklyn as our families intertwined. They now live in Rockville Centre, Long Island. His daughter, Veronica

Boyhan, a math teacher and program chair in a New York City high school, presented the following.

After Larry and I began teaching together in the late 1960s, our families became friends. We lived in the same neighborhood and spent time together, including a summer in Plattsburg when Meredith was an infant and another summer at a teaching workshop at the University of Minnesota in 1974 – the summer Nixon resigned. We shared joys and sorrows.

Larry asked me to read these remarks for him. They actually reflect much of what I was going to say, so I'll use his words:

> As longtime friends, I want people to know that Bill and his wife, Lori, had a similar type of marriage to ours. Sandy and I were what in Yiddish is *bashert* – one partner completes the other.

> As our families intertwined, your daughters, in succession, became Meredith's babysitters. And Meredith was happy when Sandy and I would go out. With Dolores she could cuddle, with Veronica she could laugh, and with Lydia she could extend her bedtime hour, no matter how logical Lydia was.

> Meredith grew into her teens and, as teens often do, she started to rebel. Sandy, as mothers do, became worried. I remember sitting in your living room seeking counsel. You gave us the best piece of advice we ever got: "Don't worry," you said. "Your values are in there someplace. It

may take time, but they'll come out in Meredith, and she'll be fine."

Now, to tell Sandy not to worry about Meredith is like telling water not to seek its own level. But, to her amazement, you were right. Meredith's self-confidence grew, and she turned into a strong, capable, agile, and gentle person. She exhibits these qualities with her family, with her career at Yahoo, and with me – especially in dealing with Sandy's illness.

The hospital system compresses time. After a while, you don't know one day from the next. Meredith became my anchor while I was adrift and we both safely allowed Sandy to complete her life with dignity. In one of my end-of-life conversations with Sandy, she told me how proud she was of her daughter. As am I.

Now, speaking for neither my father nor Larry:

I remember when Sandy was selling artwork as a side gig to supplement her teacher's salary, and she hired me to serve hors d'oeuvres and such to prospective buyers. She was probably trying to encourage me to become a waitress rather than a teacher, but I didn't listen! Regardless, this meant a lot to me – that such a refined, poised, well-educated woman had enough confidence in me to allow me to work with her. I thank you, Sandy.

~

PHIL TAMA was an educational administrator for the New York City Board of Education and lived on the same block as Sandy. His first wife, Lanni, died of cancer at an early age. He now lives in Brooklyn and Florence, Italy, with his second wife, Ellyn Toscano.

Early this June I arrived home from Florence as I have each of the last 10 years since I retired from the Department of Education. My wife, Ellyn, is the Director of New York University's program there. She works while I enjoy my permanent vacation exploring Italy and Europe. But home to me has been on Rugby Road in Ditmas Park West since I moved there in 1978 with my first wife, Lanni, and our 20-month-old son, Jordan. I remember my in-laws at the time saying, "So, you want to move to a changing neighborhood." Indeed we did, and through the years the neighborhood clearly changed for the better.

We moved into what traditionally was Old Flatbush but had been long ago divided into a number of smaller neighborhoods with Euro-sounding names like Midwood Park, Beverley Square, Fiske Terrace, and Ditmas Park. Local banks had red-lined Flatbush in the mid-1970s and fears of white flight flourished, as had been occurring in Canarsie, Hollis, and St. Albans.

Many of the beautiful turn-of-the-century Victorian-style houses needed repair because many aging homeowners could not maintain the costs of upkeep. Consequently, houses there were relatively affordable, and we were part of a new wave of

94

pioneers bent on raising families in homes with driveways, front lawns, and backyards.

Now, one of my primary tasks when I return home for the summer is to tackle the weed-infested strip of lawn at my curbside. And on a beautiful Sunday afternoon several weeks ago, I was up to my elbows in weeds and dirt when Meredith came strolling up Rugby Road with Charlie in tow on their way to a birthday party nearby. What a pleasant surprise.

Here was Meredith, whom I hadn't seen since her wedding day nine or 10 years ago, looking as radiant as ever. And a growing-up "Cha-ee," whom I'd heard so much about from Grammy Sandy. It seems that Charlie was getting a little tour of her Mommy's childhood roots.

I asked Meredith how her Mom and Dad were doing and told her I owed Sandy a call. After Sandy and Larry moved to Manhattan, Sandy and I had kept in touch, mostly by email. Hers would usually start off with "Hello from the Berkshires" or "Hello from N.Y.," and my responses would invariably start with "Ciao from Firenze" or "Greetings from Rugby Road." Meredith said they were fine – Mom was just having some tests – but her eyes said otherwise. Mindful of her daughter, she said she would pass on my well wishes to her parents.

As I watched them stroll away I was overcome with nostalgia. I was so struck by the memory of Sandy and young Meredith strolling down Rugby Road so many years ago, just as Meredith and her daughter were now; how similar Meredith, as a young mother, was to her mother, those many years ago, and how Meredith's beauty and poise called to mind the grace and elegance of her mother.

It was no surprise, then, that the Tamas and the Abramses became fast friends. Shortly after we arrived, Sheryl and David Ford moved to the block, and they were followed several years later by Ofra and Jeff Werden. Our four families took turns hosting dinner gatherings. Sandy and Larry's dinners were always exceptional.

They loved to entertain in their home. This entourage also would gather together in late January to watch the Super Bowl together. Rotating this event from house to house ended when it was decided that the Abrams house was the most enjoyable venue. Their home was always immaculate, tastefully decorated, and welcoming. I remember one year when Sandy was selling works of art from their house. Sandy had turned their home into a little museum. This only happens in Ditmas Park West.

In those early years, the neighborhood association was dormant, having lapsed as the older homeowners stopped participating. Since we had a growing nucleus of new young families, we decided to form a block association to rekindle some neighborly spirit. We engaged all 34 houses on our block to participate in activities, such as block parties, lawn sales, and annual tree plantings.

One summer evening, Larry and Sandy had the block closed off and brought in chamber musicians. This only happens in Ditmas Park West. Subsequently, Larry was able to replicate our block's success by rejuvenating the Ditmas Park West Association, which remains strong and active. When neighbors vacationed, one of us would be sure to shovel walkways, mow lawns, receive mail, and watch over their house. Our families flourished and our kids were well educated.

We celebrated birthdays, anniversaries, and graduations together, as well as work-related promotions and achievements. Occasionally we left our oasis and took off to the Adirondacks for some river rafting. But we also shared our setbacks and losses together. The untimely deaths of both Ofra and Lanni hit us the hardest. And yes, we mourned their passing together.

Everyone here today knows what a special woman Sandy was – a devoted wife and partner with Larry, a loving mother to Meredith, and most recently, a joyous grandmother to Charlie and Dexter. She was a loyal colleague and trusted friend – authentic and non-judgmental. Sandy was always in control of herself but never controlling of others. As was her way, she spared us unnecessary pain. I valued our friendship and will miss her.

~

JULIAN COHEN is an educational administrator for New York City's Department of Education in charge of developing charter schools and other new small schools. He is a distant cousin from South Africa who taught in the townships and saw the injustices of apartheid firsthand. Julian was invited to stay with Sandy and Larry when it became

apparent that the South African government would force him to serve in the military, which meant he would be forced to "control" blacks in the townships. He stayed in the U.S., became a teacher, married Rochelle, and raised a family on the upper West Side of Manhattan.

I am here to speak to Sandy's generous spirit and the bond between Larry, Meredith, and Sandy. I am Julian, and I am Larry and Sandy's cousin. Technically, I am on Larry's side of the family, and technically I am probably not exactly a cousin. Larry's father and my grandfather were brothers, so that definitely makes us related, although the technicalities of this extended family are hard to explain.

Chronologically, my connection to Sandy comes before she was a principal, when she was a teacher, a working mother to a beautiful pre-teen, and a loving partner to Larry, who was then a founding new school principal. I experienced their close-knit family firsthand because Larry, Sandy, and Meredith invited me into their home as a guest for an extended period.

This was a time for me when I was lost, wandering, in exile from South Africa, caught up in the politics of the struggle for justice against racism. I got an invitation from Larry and Sandy to come and stay in their home in Brooklyn if I needed a place to escape to.

For me, this was the most generous offer in the world, to invite a stranger into your home, a young adult whom you don't know, whose only connection is to an extended family that seemed so distantly related. But this is the heartfelt, giving, generous person that Sandy was. I know the invitation came from both Larry and Sandy, but we all know that Larry can make impetuous decisions sometimes. And so I know it was with Sandy's blessing that their invitation came, and I will never forget their patience and support for me during this strange time.

Living with Larry, Sandy, and Meredith reminded me every day of the importance of family, love, and hard work – three values that I saw exhibited and practiced in that house every day and that I learned from and tried to impart to my own family. Sandy embraced her husband and daughter in such a powerful way and held them together in what is the definition of a strong nuclear family.

For both Larry and Meredith, I saw firsthand how Sandy was the rock in their granite relationship. Sandy's reach and generosity extended so much further than her family. She was in a giving profession – teaching – and gave to her students and colleagues every day. She taught foreign language, teaching tolerance and respect for diversity. It is no wonder that she also embraced me, a stranger from another country, and made me part of her family.

I am speaking here today also on behalf of our extended family who cannot be here – although they may be virtually present, literally as well as figuratively. Larry, your sister and cousins in California, your extended family in England and South Africa, are here to support you and serve as a reminder of the strength of the bond between you and Sandy and the reach of her legacy. I am also here today as a father and husband who is inspired by the strong family foundation that you and Sandy and Meredith built.

Larry, you and Sandy have been so good to me over all these years. Your generosity has extended to my children, your interest in Luc and Khaya's accomplishments. I am so proud to be part of your extended family. We love you, Larry and Meredith, and we remember Sandy's generosity and strength. It will live on in your family through Charlie and Dexter and the generations to come. Sandy would have wanted it this way.

~

JANE KRAMER (reading on Meredith's behalf) is a social-work supervisor at Lighthouse Guild International, where she oversees nurses, social workers, and a palliative-care team. Jane and Meredith met in the second grade and have remained friends ever since. Jane lives in Nyack, N.Y.

I met Meredith, Sandy, and Larry when I was seven. They included me in everything they did, and I quickly felt like family. That was 35 years ago; the feeling hasn't changed. That is perhaps why Meredith asked that I read this letter to her mom on her behalf:

Mom,

I am not sure how to write this without asking you to proofread and perfect my words. I am not sure how to call your home phone number without saying, "Is Mommy there?" I am simply not sure how not to have you in my life.

I am your daughter and you are alive in me. Your strength, your character, your humor, your sarcasm, and, of course, your lack of any desire to ever cook anything. I am honored to have you as my mother. And I am privileged to have you as my dear friend. Your unconditional love and support have guided me through my everything. I am at a complete loss for words on how we ended up here today. But there are a few important things that I want to say and promise you:

I will always work to find happiness.

I will always strive to make you proud.

I will always make sure that Charlie and Dexter know how much you adore them.

And I will always ensure that the love of your life, my wonderful and amazing father, is surrounded by the love of our family.

Mom, with these pledges to you, I just ask that you rest and be at peace. You will live on in my heart and all of my memories, always.

~

HELEN ADLER is a clinical social worker and practicing therapist in New York City. Her parents

were Holocaust survivors who knew Sandy's parents. Their upbringing as children of survivors had many parallels. She and her husband, Elliot, were neighbors of Sandy's in the Berkshires.

I first met Sandy when she was three years old and I was four, at our beloved cousin Mildred Belsky's home. Sandy was American born. I was born in a displaced persons hospital in Austria, which was no doubt similar to the kind of camp at which her parents, Willie and Edith, had met. My maiden name was Helen Ofman, and hers was Sandy Hoffman.

My father, Mayer, and her father, Willie, were born in Radomsko, Poland, where there were many Hoffmans and Ofmans. Most of them were butchers or in the leather business. Refugees from Radomsko have a special section at the New Montefiore Cemetery. Whenever I visit my parents' graves, I stop at Willie and Edith's and leave a stone.

Our parents were Holocaust survivors. Although I didn't know this as a child, we were in a category of children who would become known as "Children of Survivors." Before the 1970s, the word "Holocaust" had not yet been coined to refer to the Nazis' attempt to systematically exterminate the Jewish people. My parents simply referred to themselves as "we who lived through the war."

Fellow survivors became each other's families, social world, and safety net. My mother was pained by what she felt was a rejecting attitude from American Jews, who were not welcoming and who didn't want to hear the details of what happened to them. Sandy's family was part of a close-knit group of three families that lived near each other in Brooklyn.

They socialized on a weekly basis, vacationed together, and cared for each other's children. I remember long, hot subway rides on many a Sunday afternoon all the way from the Grand Concourse to Cousin Mildred's house. Mildred was emotionally important to both Sandy and me. At that time, she had no children of her own, and we were like surrogate daughters. Though we lived far apart, she kept us connected through stories about one another.

Survivors coped with their painful past in two major but different ways. Sandy's parents and my parents clearly exemplified the differences. Hers, Edith and Willie, were committed to sheltering their children from the knowledge and burden of what had happened. My parents, on the other hand, couldn't contain their traumas, and I remember how, when their friends came to visit, they became deeply immersed in recalling their suffering. But regardless of how any parents dealt with their pain, none of their children could remain unaffected by the enormity of their experience.

Sandy's parents later told her stories that communicated lessons in courage and endurance, as well as danger, fear, and fate. Her mother passed as a gentile to save her life.

One day on a train, she was recognized by a man, a thief, who could have exposed her Jewish identity. He did not. Instead, he said, "I am a thief, and I have already robbed you three times. I owe you and I will let you go." Posing as a gentile, she found work for a Nazi officer. At the end of the war he was most horrified to learn that he had inadvertently saved a Jewish life.

At risk to himself, Sandy's father sold jewelry for other Jews who desperately tried to raise the necessary funds to escape. He never charged a fee for this work. Years later, at a special ceremony in Florida, he was honored for his courageous actions on their behalf. Sandy's parents' values of courage, devotion, and hopefulness were embodied in Sandy's life. More than anything, survivors wished for a better world for their children. In the spirit of *tikkun olam,* Sandy strove to make the world a better place by becoming an esteemed educator of children. My path led me to become a psychotherapist.

It is ironic that Sandy and I began our lives in the same community of survivors and were reunited years later in a completely different community, Indian Lake. We discovered that we shared a love for exotic travel, as well as intense curiosity about people of foreign cultures.

Speaking of coincidence, a few years ago my husband, Elliot, and I, were in a canoe on Inle Lake in Myanmar, approaching our floating hotel. By chance, standing on the dock were Larry and Sandy, waving a warm welcome, so many miles from home.

With that special memory, I wave goodbye to my friend.

~

JODIE COHEN was an assistant principal and protégé of Sandy when Sandy was the principal of James Madison. Today, Jodie is the principal of Madison and resides in Brooklyn with her husband, Matt.

To me, Madison High School will never be the same. There are many days that I will just sit and think in the principal's office and ask myself, What would Sandy have done? Sitting at the very same desk that she did is an honor. As the principal of Madison, she dedicated her heart and soul to what was most important, and that was the children. The students knew who she was and looked forward to performing on the stage to see her sitting in her seat – the first seat in the auditorium.

I was so fortunate to be trained by Sandy. She took me under her wing and enabled me to follow in her footsteps. As the principal of Madison High School, there is not a day that goes by without me smiling because I know I just did something the way that Sandy showed me how. She never gave anyone the answers; she would sit in a chair and allow you to "think it through." It was amazing how her simple questions allowed one to figure out a solution without her ever really telling you exactly how to do it.

I remember the time that I was helping to clear the lobby, and I got a bit loud. Sandy came over to me and asked me if raising my voice helped the situation. To this day, when I raise my voice to speak to children I realize I just made a mistake. Sandy never raised her voice but always managed to command attention from the whole room. The students respected her and admired her style. When there were school dances – she allowed the first dance that ever happened at the school – she would be on the dance floor among the students. She made everyone in the school community feel like they were a part of her team.

A few days ago, Lucille, one of Sandy's secretaries, shared an email with me that she had sent to Larry, and in that email she described how Sandy was not just a leader but a friend. Lucille has never known anyone she respects and admires as much as Sandy. She was intelligent and poised, a strong and fair leader.

When Sandy retired, a big part of us was missing, a third to be exact, and no one has ever replaced her, or ever will. Lori was another of Sandy's secretaries, but to those who truly knew them, they were the "dream team" (Sandy, Lori, and Lucille). Another very dear friend of Sandy and a colleague, Sheila Hanley, could not be here today because she is in Ireland – which I am sure Sandy would be happy to hear. When Sheila came to me at Madison to share the sad news that Sandy was ill, I stopped her from crying and said Sandy is an amazing woman and we must hold on to that. We also both stopped and looked at each and realized that it was Sandy who had brought us together.

Sheila shared some words with me about what Sandy meant and I would like to share it with all of you:

"The multitude of diamonds on a tiara can never outshine the vibrancy and warmth of Sandy's personality. She had a quiet knack for nurturing talent and ideas. Just being with her in interviews taught me how to judge a person's potential and talent. Not just instructional strategies or the new social studies assessments, but the necessary human qualities that make a person more than a teaching machine."

[Jodie remembers her interview for the Assistant Principal job with Sandy as more of a conversation between acquaintances than an interview. – L.A.]

Sandy had a gentle way of making you feel comfortable in a strange environment. And it was a strange environment since she was trained at the more progressive Edward R. Murrow High School. She asked me, "Who was your favorite teacher? Why? What do you consider the most important characteristic in an administrator?" When she asked me if I thought I would make a good administrator, I responded yes.

She thought she was a good administrator, too, because she was married, as was I. She stated if one could negotiate the trials of a marriage, being an administrator was a piece of cake. Through that interview, I received the opportunity to become an administrator, devoted to James Madison High School, but more importantly I received the golden opportunity for friendship with a beloved woman, Sandy.

A few nights ago, I was on the phone with my friend, Aaron Perez, also a principal, and we were speaking about what an amazing woman Sandy was. She always held her head high and made everyone feel like a part of the team. Aaron shared stories of their trip to China right after Sandy retired and how Sandy made the trip most memorable. He reflected on the many conversations they had and how she gave him so many pearls of wisdom. I look back and realize how lucky we all are to have been touched by the true golden knight – Sandy Abrams. I would like to share an excerpt from *A Woman of Valor* by Eric S. Kingston, that truly defines Sandy:

> *A woman of valor makes the world change*
> *Her strength is the content that guides through the days ...*
> *For only her heart will know the depths of her soul*
> *That nurtures and blossoms and forever unfolds ...*
> *Yes,*
> *A woman of valor makes the world change*

~

ELLEN VICTOR and MARIE VIOLA, former assistant principals and teachers of English in New York City, bonded with Sandy through The Freeman Foundation's Educational Scholars' Program to study in depth and travel to foreign counties. They remained friends – and that was even after their travels to Japan, China, Mongolia, Tibet, and Korea.

ELLEN VICTOR: Tennessee Williams wrote, "Make voyages! – Attempt them! – There's nothing else." Sandy and Larry lived a life filled with unforgettable voyages, but Sandy was not merely a tourist; she was a traveler in the best sense of the word. She was interested in the wider world, in discovering new places, learning new ideas, meeting new people. Although

Sandy and Larry traveled to many European cities, even taking Meredith with them, I knew her as a traveling companion to China and Japan when we met Hazel Greenberg. Hazel was a teacher who worked with a program called New York and the World. Through this organization, she acquired grants that enabled New York City teachers to travel to Asia to better understand this part of the world. Sandy was an intrepid tourist whose quick wit and warm smile made her a wonderful companion with whom to share these new experiences.

I remember the night in Japan when Sandy and another teacher decided to attend a Japanese bath. The rest of us were too afraid to go. Not Sandy. She went into the unknown and was so relaxed that she fell asleep. After a time, she awoke to realize that everyone else except she and Lynn Greenfield had left. Sandy and Lynn, having only small wash cloths for cover, walked through the bath to change into their clothes, in front of a group of stunned Japanese. Returning to the inn, they shared their hysterical experiences with us. Another time in Japan we all remember was when Sandy and Larry got up earlier than the rest of us to observe a cormorant fisherman. Sandy had read about this unique fishing technique in her studies of Japan. She and Larry got up early, went to the river, and waited until dawn to see the birds fish. The cormorants are attached to a string, and they dive into the waters, bringing back fish in their beaks to the fisherman on shore.

We all benefited as Sandy and Larry shared with us what they had seen and learned. Sandy was not only a great traveler; she was also a great travel agent. She would undertake research and would willingly share the information. She would always find the best houseboat in Cochin, the most beautiful hotel in India, the most unique holy day in Bali, and the newest culinary hit in the Berkshires. All of this information was shared with all who knew her.

No matter where she went, she made friends. Whether it was among the teachers she traveled with, the schoolchildren she visited, the camel sellers she met, Sandy was a great ambassador for the U.S. She had a special gift for listening to people, being excited to learn about their lives, and being willing to share their customs.

St. Augustine wrote: "The world is a book and those who do not travel read only one page." Sandy's life was a vast library.

MARIE VIOLA: Yes, Sandy's life was a vast library, and because I was lucky enough to be her friend, I, like so many others, was the beneficiary of that vast knowledge. In addition to Japan, she, Larry, and I traveled with our friends Hazel Greenberg and Linda Arkin to Mongolia, Tibet, and Iran. I remember that in Mongolia we were invited to the yurt of a local herdsman. In an act of Mongolian hospitality, we were each given a glass of fermented mare's milk to drink. Sandy, ever the gracious guest, did not blink an eye and accepted the most unappealing drink with the great Sandy charm.

But we soon discovered that we were not only visiting a yurt; we were to spend a few freezing-cold nights sleeping in one, on a magnificent, crystal-clear lake in the wilds of Mongolia. Did Sandy complain? No way! She saw only the beauty of the lake and felt only the warmth of the people. And so, on to

Tibet, where one afternoon we happened to be in Lhasa, the capital, on market day. Sandy suggested that we leave the group for a bit and go off to the market where one could buy almost anything, including a yak. Well, it didn't take us very long to realize that most of the Tibetans were buying the local hooch, and we and the children were the only sober ones there. Sandy being Sandy, she continued to smile and charm the children while steering clear of the drunks!

As Ellen said, Sandy was a great ambassador for the U.S. At our hotel in Esfahan, Iran, in its beautiful outdoor garden cafe, she and Larry engaged a young Iranian woman in conversation. Not only did they invite her to return the following evening as their guest; they maintained an email correspondence with her for some time after.

At this point I would be most remiss if I did not mention the fact that only Sandy could be effortlessly lovely wearing a headscarf and covered from head to toe in the 90-plus degree weather of Iran. Sandy was beautiful both inside and out. Yes, we were all introduced to the beauty and power of Asia by our dear friend Hazel. Hazel may have planted the seed, but Sandy made it flower.

My last afternoon with Sandy was on April 24th. We spent it touring the Oceania galleries at the Metropolitan Museum of Art. Witnessing Sandy's ever-present thirst for knowledge and her insightful questions for our guide, I knew then that I would one day visit that part of the South Pacific. And when I do, Sandy's spirit will be with me. It was during lunch that day that she told me she couldn't believe she hadn't yet taken Dexter, age two, to the museum. She said, "I had Charlie crawling around the museum before age two." To this day, because of Sandy, Charlie loves museums. Her favorite is when Grammy shows her the palace rooms of period furniture at the Met. Sandy wanted her grandchildren to have the gift of curiosity about life and art in all its wonders.

The Buddhists would say Sandy had a very old and a very, very beautiful soul.

~

STEPHEN FELDMAN was the founder of Advanced Provider Systems, Inc., and at present is a practicing psychologist in Colts Neck, N.J. He and his wife, Libby, live in Morganville, N.J.

Libby and I met Sandy and Larry in 1989, the year that they built their house in Indian Lake Estates in the Berkshires. That was one year after we had done the same. We all quickly recognized and appreciated our compatibility, and over the years we became closer and closer.

Sandy has now been tragically taken from us. Our hearts are broken. You see, Sandy was not your average person. She was physically striking, warm, charismatic, athletic, intelligent, funny, deep, and wise. She had a sophistication about her that was devoid of snobbishness. She was very accepting of differences, and, indeed, she seemed fascinated by the diversity in peoples and in cultures. She loved planning for travel, and she was very detail-oriented in her preparations. Her memory for the names of small towns she had visited, esoteric foods she had tasted, and words in the many foreign tongues of the diverse places she had visited was absolutely astounding. Dan Scher, a good friend, described her as a travel *balabusta*. I concur with that description, which uses a term for which no English translation can capture its full meaning. Suffice it to say that she was a very competent planner and traveler.

Sandy was also very "socially versatile." She could talk to anyone, regardless of their station in life, their level of intellect, their education, and their ethnicity. And she really listened. As you spoke, you could see how intently she concentrated. I have heard Bill Clinton described as someone who could focus on you so intently as you talked to him that it made you feel as if you were the most important person in the world.

Well, Sandy was like that, too. I always felt that she really "got" me. Sandy had depth. She saw the meaning in things and in people; she saw beyond surface information; she could really read a person. And she could really read a book, so much so that I loved talking to her about any book that we had both recently read. She always saw things that made the author's words seem more fascinating than I had found them before our discussion.

But the image of Sandy that most readily pops into my mind when I think about her is her sitting on a beach chair at Indian Lake's Forest Beach, with a Sunday *New York Times* crossword puzzle in her lap. Larry is next to her, also sitting in a beach chair and reading a different section of the paper. Libby and I are walking down the tree-canopied path that heads downhill from the road to the beach, and we are schlepping our chairs and a bag, filled with towels, keys, wallets, books, and a plastic storage bag containing cherries or watermelon. Once we sit down, perhaps to Sandy and Larry's chagrin (though they never showed it), the reading and the puzzle-solving stop. It's probably Libby who begins talking with Larry, throwing in an occasional sample of humorous and sometimes not-so-humorous sarcasm. He alone laughs at both.

Gradually our conversation becomes more mutually contributory and meaningful. Eventually it becomes funny; sometimes hilarious. And that's where I can so vividly see Sandy's smile and hear her laugh. I remember the heartiness of that laugh, reflecting the depths within from which it sprang. Sandy's laugh was contagious. Sometimes she had trouble stopping it. Sometimes I couldn't stop laughing, either. And that's how I picture Sandy – on Forest Beach, laughing.

Just the other day, Jeanette Leimer, an Indian Lake resident, told Libby that she remembers her first meeting with Sandy. It was also at Forest Beach. She described her as a statuesque young woman wearing a bikini. Yes, in retrospect, I too remember that white bikini. Actually, I don't think Sandy ever outgrew it.

Over the past few years, across the lake from Forest Beach on Boulder Beach, our crew of 10 or so couples began to have wonderfully enjoyable little late-afternoon picnics. Often at the center of these celebrations were Sandy and Larry. After a few glasses of Larry's carefully selected wine, or Jeanette Katz's mysterious Italian liqueurs, Sandy's laughter would begin to grow. Its contagiousness, and the aforementioned libations, would eventually ensure that the laughing disease spread to us all. Those were wonderful times and, in my mind's eye, I see Sandy laughing and loving and full of life and vitality.

And now she is gone. Except for the memories and the lasting influences she has had on us all, she is no longer with us. She was clearly her own person, yet why do I have so much trouble picturing her separate from Larry? It was always Sandy and Larry, or Larry and Sandy, or the Abramses. Sandy was never a person in a vacuum. She was always a part of Sandy and Larry, even when he was not present. She and her best friend, her lover, her sweetheart and fellow traveler through life, shared a universe. I will get used to seeing Larry alone, but I will always appreciate his tie to Sandy.

And, of course, Larry will be facing a very difficult but unavoidable challenge – that of adapting to his loss and developing and accepting a markedly changed view of himself and a changed view of the world.

The essence that is Sandy will live on through her family. She is part of the woman that Meredith has become. She is in her biology, and she is in her psychology. And her essence has been passed on to her grandchildren – Charlie, who reflects Sandy's beauty, sense of humor, intelligence, and zest for life; and Dexter, whose strong will, *joie de vivre*, courage, and mischievousness reflect the wonderful woman who was their grandmother.

We will all miss you, Sandy. But the strength, pragmatism, and resilience that you demonstrated throughout your life as you confronted unanticipated tragedies will, over time and in a natural fashion, be channeled through you to the family you left behind, such that your memory will bring a smile to their faces in spite of the emptiness in their hearts. You have left an indelible mark on all your family and friends.

Libby and I will think of you often; we will remember your laugh and your spirit. We will recall the good times and, on occasion, we will cry as we remember your passing. But we, like everyone else here, have been privileged to have known you and to have been touched by you.

Sandy, we love you. Rest in peace.

~

ALICE NEUFELD is an interior designer who bonded with Sandy instantly when they met in the Berkshires. Later, they traveled to Italy together. She and her husband, Max, now live in San Miguel de Allende, Mexico.

After all the instructions, both verbal and written, we took off in our rented Mercedes station wagon for the historic walled Tuscan village of Greve. Sounds like a perfect plan, right until we came to the sign *Prese di Fabbrica* (factory outlets). To any woman, this sign says, "Turn here. Gucci and Prada ahead."

So all our great plans to see this picturesque ancient town were scrapped in a split second just as we got to the fork in the road. Sandy was the driver. She was always good at decision making. When we returned to the hotel, parking our huge car practically in the lobby of the hotel, the concierge asked how we liked Greve. With a wink to each other, our arms loaded with shopping bags, Sandy said it was picturesque and we loved it – so much we might need to return.

And ... we never got to Greve.

Sandy and I spent a glorious nine days in Montecatini 11 years ago, just the two of us. So that being said, two close friends, happy to be together anywhere – but especially in Italy – no rules or requirements except to have fun. What could have been better? Except ... we never got to Greve.

Instead, we woke up each morning to plan the day's adventure. One day we drove to Sienna. Okay, we saw the Palio, where the horses race each year; the Cathedral, the main square. But what drew our undivided attention were Max Mara and the black suit in the window. We rushed in to try it on, but they only had one suit – can't recall which of us it fit, but definitely only one. The salesperson saw that we would settle for nothing else. She called all the Max Mara stores nearby and found two black suits for us in Florence.

The fact that it was getting dark could not stop us (we were on a mission). We found the store – was there any doubt? – and left the car somewhere; we would worry about this later. The people in the store were waiting for us. Yes, we bought the same black suits. (You're allowed to do this if they are black.) Just as the dressmaker was finishing the necessary alterations, we spotted a fabulous gown and velvet cape – perfect for Sandy. I insisted Sandy try it on. Well, of course, she could have stopped traffic, she looked so gorgeous. I talked her into buying it. Of course, you would get a lot of use out of a gown and velvet cape. Who wouldn't? So that, too, was delivered to the hotel. We were giddy with excitement! We each never wore these suits without thinking of the other, and of course we still have them.

But … we never got to Greve.

But we did go to the spa at the hotel. Montecatini is a spa town. So, we decided to relax after the shopping adventure. We made spa appointments at the hotel for the indoor whirlpool at the hotel followed by a massage. The rules of the pool were "naked and showercap" required. So, here we are in this pool, staring at each other in disbelief (Sandy could see better than I because I had removed my contact lenses) and she said nonchalantly, with that captivating smile and those twinkling eyes, "I don't think I have ever seen you in the water before!" Who could ever forget that scene?

But … we never got to Greve.

Instead, we decided to go to Fiesole to have a great lunch. I don't remember how we got to the town. What I will never forget is the endless stone road we walked up, feeling completely lost in the woods, until we came to a few stone buildings in a clearing at the top of what seemed to us a mountain.

We walked into the building and proceeded in the direction of the voices we heard. We were in the kitchen of a school.

Sandy explained as best she could that we were lost on our way to the Villa San Michele in Fiesole. Sandy did the communicating with the cook, who somehow understood her and phoned the bus driver, who was at home having lunch.

When the driver and the bus arrived, we realized this school was a kindergarten – the bus was for kids three feet tall. To the bus driver, this was an incredible scene – two American ladies lost on a stone road looking for the Villa San Michele. So he took us in the little school bus to the restaurant, and that is how we arrived at the Villa San Michele; the concierge is still talking about us.

But ... we never got to Greve.

Instead, we had nine days together of laughter and joy neither of us ever forgot – the ultimate bonding experience for both of us. We so enjoyed being together. We got looped at a local restaurant and told each other secrets we thought we would never reveal – and didn't. We called Libby in New Jersey from our room one night – out of nowhere we remembered her phone number and we had a phone card. We were excited telling her about the stairway to nowhere in our room, where we added our shopping bags each night until they filled the stairs. We had signals to each other on the bus; #6 meant you'd better move away from the person coming your way.

But ... we never got to Greve.

Instead, we came home filled with these treasured memories and created some more along the way. "How was it?" I asked

Sandy while driving to Long Island on the Grand Central Parkway.

"OK," said Sandy. "He was funny."

"OK," I said. "That's a plus, I think. Would you go back?"

"I guess so. If he's here," Sandy said.

I suddenly realized that I was talking about the new gynecologist she went to the day before, and she was talking about hearing Carl Reiner at the 92nd St Y. We've giggled about that experience ever since.

Sandy was retired. We had one day a week set aside for an adventure, like walking from 89th Street to Soho or accidentally coming upon, and joining, a group of Japanese ladies at a tea ceremony in a small museum. We visited Sotheby's and Christie's, Sandy copying an Ellsworth Kelly painting for the living room of their apartment. It looked easy enough, so she enthusiastically took on the job.

For a month we were in the Zimbabwe sculpture business, carrying around stone sculptures in the trunk of the car. Sandy was always a willing accomplice to these schemes. We shared our concerns for our children, our futures, our dreams. Sandy's amazing gift of listening and not judging was unique to her. Of course, being warm and loving, sincere, caring, brilliant, sensitive, sweet, funny, athletic, beautiful, and tall didn't hurt. Sandy is the most incredible woman I have ever known. She had it all wrapped into one incredibly beautiful package. Larry,

Meredith, Drew, Charlie, and Dexter – and everyone whose lives she touched – how lucky all are to have had this fabulous woman part of us. The gift of memory is how to keep her alive. Sandy, you and I never got to Greve together, but we all grieve for you – now and always.

~

CAROLE LONDON and FRAN BOONIN were elementary school teachers in Setauket, Long Island, who team-taught together and not only survived, but enjoyed it. People say they – and their husbands, Stu and Bob – are all joined at the hip. Today the couples live on Long Island – but in separate homes.

Some things stay with you, shape you, indelibly imprint on your heart, mind, and soul. Ever so rarely that imprint comes by way of a person – a unique person: Sandy. We are all incredibly fortunate to have had her in our lives for the time we did, although far too brief. Our memories are vivid and reflect back to us like the shimmering sunlight as it skips off Indian Lake, a place Sandy so loved. There were countless times we sat by the calm water and laughed about the little things in our lives. Sandy loved to laugh. There were discussions about our children, their lives, and then their children's lives, our grandchildren's. We remember her sitting in the shallow water, with Meredith and Charlie, being a special Mom and Grammy.

We talked about so many things – serious issues, some trivial, some funny, some sad, always important in the moment. Plans, places traveled – Sandy could remember almost to the minute where she was and what she did 10 years ago, while the rest of us couldn't remember what we had for breakfast. Books, food, so many topics are all part of the collage of memories. Her quiet confidence was always present in the background with her humor, intellect, intensity, and wisdom. Each time we would get together, it began with her welcoming smile that lit up her face and those around her, like a ray of sunshine. When we had not seen each other for a while, there was always that hug, the one that said, "I really care about you."

She was a truly unique person, so rare to find. Sandy was the complete package, with beauty inside and out – intellect, charm, wit, humor, humility, inquisitiveness, caring, and charisma all wrapped up in one special human being. Because of these qualities, she will never be gone from us. The indelible imprint will keep her with us for the rest of our lives. For Larry, Meredith, and all their loved ones, the hole in their hearts and lives will eventually fill with warm memories of a wonderfully unique person whose gift to all of us was her being Sandy. She will never be gone from our lives – indelibly imprinted.

This is adapted from *The Prophet* by Kahlil Gibran:

> *And let your best be for your friend.*
> *If she must know the ebb of your tide, let her know its flood also.*
> *For what is your friend that you should seek her with hours*
>   *to kill?*
> *Seek her always with hours to live.*
> *For it is hers to fill your need, but not your emptiness.*
> *And in the sweetness of friendship let there be laughter,*

and sharing of pleasures.
For in the dew of little things the heart finds its morning
and is refreshed.

~

JEANETTE KATZ was the president, and is now on
the board of directors, of G-III Apparel Group,
which produces and distributes such brands as
Andrew Mark, Calvin Klein, Bass, and Vilebrequin.
She was a Berkshire neighbor for 25 years and a new
friend for six years, eventually becoming Sandy's
bridge partner. She is an adjunct faculty member at
the Fashion Institute of Technology's School of
Graduate Studies. Jeanette and her husband, Carl,
live in Hastings-on-Hudson, N.Y.

Sandy, my friend. It was 40 days from the Friday that Larry
called to say my friend was up all night with some sort of
stomach virus and they would not play golf ... until we received
the terrible, terrible news that she had left us.

During one of the many phone calls, emails, and text
messages we exchanged, I told Larry that for many years in
Becket, we had been neighbors and acquaintances, casually
chatting on the tennis court or at the lake. But in the last
three years we had become friends. To make friends at this
time in our lives was a rare and special gift. Sandy and I
chose to befriend each other.

As many of you know, Sandy and I were bridge partners, and
both a little nuts about bridge – she the more intellectual and

analytical, me the more intuitive and risk taking; we made a good team. We took classes together, met to study and plan strategies. We often played twice a week. My friend and I would read and analyze each new convention. Then we would meet to discuss our interpretations, and when she felt she fully understood it she would say, "Partner, I think we are ready to add that." And we did.

We spent a lot of time together. We shared some silly triumphs and some hysterically funny moments. We actually came in First Overall in a tournament for new bridge players, earning nine-tenths of a masterpoint. We worked hard for that fractional masterpoint. Sandy laughed and laughed when I Photoshopped and framed our winning results into a bridge magazine cover for her. We giggled like schoolgirls when the old geezers in San Miguel Bridge Club flirted with us, the new girls in town. We laughed out loud at some of the mixed nuts we met in our bridge games in Great Barrington. But in and around all this time spent, our friendship blossomed and deepened.

We shared our hopes and concerns. My friend listened to my anxiety about a rough patch Ben was having and my worries about my grandson Marcus.

My friend was a proud and private person, but she did on occasion let us see inside the 50-year love affair with that guy she lovingly called Turtle in moments when she felt truly at ease. Sandy was proud of Meredith's accomplishments at Yahoo, describing in detail a white-on-white installation at Lincoln Center. She was delighted in watching Dexter grow, and in her twice-weekly travels to Brooklyn to be with him. But there was no brighter twinkle in my friend's eyes than one recent Monday afternoon as she described in detail the pinafore Charlie had worn to see *Aladdin,* and how her unbraided hair was tousled and flowing. It was not only Charlie's beauty she marveled at, but also the way Charlie compared and contrasted the movie version of *Aladdin* to the Broadway show. Does this remind you of anyone we know?

My friend was never much interested in clothes or shopping but managed to have a sense of style and elegance second to none. Sandy once complimented me on a sweater, and I told her about the brand Vince. She amazed me by finding a shop in her neighborhood and getting the salesperson to take her into "the back room" where the sale items were. Then she told me where to find Vince on sale online.

Her approach to shopping was, as in all things, well researched, purposeful, and result-oriented. My friend recently took up golf and turned to me one afternoon and said, "Can you believe at our age we are learning not one but two new things?" Sandy's lifelong love of learning was not limited just to the intellectual side, but included yoga, tennis, and golf. My friend was terrific to hang out with because she never tired of learning and discovering something new. I've had an anchor on my chest for the last few weeks and I cannot yet comprehend that I will not see my friend again.

To make a friend this late in life is a rare and special gift. Carl helped me understand why I was feeling so lost by showing me a column by David Brooks of *The New York Times* in which he observes how much our consciousness is shaped by people around us: "Each close friend brings out a version of yourself that you could not bring out on your own. When your close friend dies, you are not only losing the friend, you are losing the version of your personality that he or she elicited." (See www.nytimes.com/2014/07/11/opinion/david-brooks-baseball-or-soccer.html.)

Thank you for the gift of friendship that I will cherish forever.

I am comforted that the flowers I sent made you smile and that I did get to hear your voice. My heart aches for Larry, Meredith, and the children. But my heart also aches for my friend and the version of myself who I will not see again.

~

LENNY LEVINE is the co-founder of Legion Paper, a company that designs and distributes fine art and photographic paper internationally. He and his wife, Sherry, became new Berkshire friends of ours when they painted their house a lovely shade of blue, which offended the sensibilities of some of the more rigid people in the community. They reside in Manhattan.

Some people have such an amazing vitality, such an electric consciousness, such a lifelong love affair with the world that when they stop breathing, it's like a wind dying, like the waning and disappearing of a light. That wind and light was Sandy. This is a sad day for all of us who were privileged to have known her and Larry as a couple – in my opinion, the perfect couple who complemented each other so much that all of us wanted to be in their company so some of what they had together could rub off on us as a couple. In my opinion, the perfect couple who complemented each other.

Sandy had a genuineness about her that made you want to listen to her observations and opinions about everything from travel (100 countries, really) to the Clinton Global Initiative. She was just plain interesting. Aside from her intellect, she and Larry had a sweetness and humor that made me feel more accomplished being around them. If I had an opinion about something and they agreed with me, I felt smarter. If they complimented me on something I was wearing, I felt better dressed ... on and on.

We spent time this past winter in San Miguel de Allende, Mexico, and I thought I had rented the perfect house ... until I had dinner and cocktails at their house. It was more perfect. I smiled in awe. That same evening the dinner guests were sitting on their upper patio, drinking margaritas and toasting each other for a life well lived. The company, laughter, food, discussions, and incredible views were cherished by us all. And yes, I believe it revolved around Sandy and Larry, who were gatherers of special friends – as witnessed by all of us here today to pay tribute to a dear friend who will be missed more than she could ever have known in life. Sherry and I were late to the Abrams's party, but in the seven or so years we were fortunate to have known them as a couple, we wanted to spend time under their canopy of intelligence and worldliness. Carl and Jeanette Katz and Sherry and I had seen what we thought was the worst performance in the history of the Jacobs Pillow Dance Festival, and when we told Sandy about it, she and Larry had seen it and absolutely loved it. We couldn't understand how they could have seen the same show and come away with this opinion. Then, as they would often do, they explained in detail what we seemingly had missed.

Normally, either Jeanette or I would argue our points, but their way of seeing life made you wonder what you were missing and what else there was in such an interesting way that you wanted more of it and them. If you wanted to know about what was the best place to eat in Bhutan, you just asked and then made a reservation the next time you happened to be in Bhutan. If you wanted to plan an exotic cruise, you just asked them. How about which country was the most fascinating for photographers? Yup, just ask them.

Sandy's thirst for everything was seemingly never-ending. Tennis, golf lessons, bridge, etc. On and on it went. Their passports were always full and their life together seemed to be adding more passport pages.

I ask you all to look around this room and see all of their friends paying tribute to someone so special that our hearts are broken. There will be a huge void without our friend. Look around and please remember to tell your loved ones and best friends how much they mean to you while it can be heard. It's beautiful to say and even more beautiful to hear. Larry, I tell you that you're not alone, and you are loved by me and so many others. When someone you love becomes a memory, the memory becomes a treasure. Those we love don't go away; their treasure walks beside you every day. Sandy, our friend, we will all see you later. Rest in peace knowing you made a difference.

~

Barbara Weinstein: During the 40 days of what turned out to be Sandy's terminal illness, she experienced a loss of control and, by extension, dignity, which were her hallmarks. Witnessing this was devastating for Larry and Meredith. As we know, his love for Sandy knew no bounds, so in Larry's characteristic way he developed a mantra for alleviating the profound fear and disorientation Sandy would experience on a regular basis:

> You are in a safe place in The Hospital, only 12 blocks from
> our apartment. If you look out the window, you have a
> view of the park. From our window at home, I can see the
> big black building where you are. The nurse and a health
> aide are with you to keep you safe. I love you, Meredith
> loves you, Charlie loves you, and Dexter loves you.

Thank you, Sandy, for all that you have taught us. Facing your death and reminiscing about the wonderful life you shared with Larry gives life a new meaning to so many of us.

Shalom chavera. Goodbye, our friend.

5. Afterwards

MEL BROOKS WON'T REMEMBER this story, but he was my neighbor in Manhattan. Since his wife Anne Bancroft died, he no longer lives in my building and now is somewhere in California. When Sandy and I saw them in the lobby or elevator we would exchange greetings. We never wanted to intrude on their celebrity. You could see by looking at them they were pleasant people who loved each other very much, and that was all we needed to know.

One pleasant spring day, Sandy and I did have a sustained chat with Mel under the brown awning of our building. We told him we were looking forward to seeing *Young Frankenstein* on Broadway. He responded that he was working on the play and at this point did not know if he was crazy or not to undertake this project at his stage in life.

He told us he was going to a restaurant on the East side of Manhattan called Peking Duck House. "You know," he added, "where the ducks come from." We told him we were going to a fish restaurant on the West Side. He responded, "Ah, the West Side slumming?" With laughter we departed for our respective restaurants.

Several months earlier, I bumped into Mel in our lobby, waiting for an elevator. He looked somewhat disheveled, not sporting his usual turned-out causal look. He was carrying plastic shopping bags filled with toilet paper and other supplies from our local Duane Reade drugstore. He wanted to talk and opened the conversation with the customary, "How are you?" I am sure he didn't know my name but recognized a neighbor's face. We chatted for five minutes about the most mundane things that neighbors chat about: the weather, the building, the neighborhood, etc. We missed several elevators recounting the small details of life until we finally wished each other a good day.

What I discovered later from one of our concierges, who knows everything that happens in the building, is that Anne Bancroft was dying of cancer and Mel was personally caring for her in his apartment. He loved her and wanted to do everything he could for her as they said their goodbyes. I surmised this because years later I read a *New York Times* article where the reporter was asking Mel about his career. The reporter asked a question like, "It must have been very difficult for you when your wife was ill. How did you handle it?" Mel responded, "Some things we don't talk about." The reporter reverted to career questions, which Mel answered easily.

At the elevator, Mel was searching for some type of normality in conversation. The pressure of watching the demise of a loved one, while you try to give her the best care possible and know you don't want her to suffer if there is no chance for recovery, is earth shattering.

You crave the normality of everyday life. You try to function with people even though a cloud has descended upon your brain. It is a battle, similar to post-traumatic stress disorder. You are fighting to keep your loved one alive. And once she passes, you struggle to keep the memories safe from voyeuristic invaders.

Now I understood the significance of our elevator conversation. I was searching for the same type of normality when Sandy was in The Hospital. I was trying to stabilize my world. When you deal with situations where everything spins out of control, you grab at the nearest straw, hoping it will support you. Much of the grieving process is like grabbing at straws. Some support you for a while, some don't. It is important to let go of those that don't.

Anger is a part of the grieving process. I was angry at the inept pain management Sandy experienced time and time again until she was mercifully admitted into The Hospice. I still see her writhing in pain when the epidural was disconnected or when the pain cocktails were not administered in the right proportions or in a timely fashion. I was angry that, had this rapidly moving disease been diagnosed and treated earlier, maybe the damage to Sandy's central nervous system could have been reversed, and I would have her back again. I was angry that doctors kept on giving me hope for the next treatment – and the next treatment after that – as a way to save her.

The exception was Dr. Torres, the thoracic surgeon, who had the guts and humanity to tell me, "I can remove the tumor, but I can't tell you that will cure her symptoms." I was angry that Sandy hadn't been fed over the Fourth of July weekend until a feeding tube, something expressly refused in her living will, was offered as the next treatment. She'd had an appetite on Friday, but with the sedation, it had vanished by Monday. I was angry that my daughter and I had to advocate so hard for her right to die with dignity, and the doctors did not know that her living will was part of her medical record. I was angry at the emergency room doctor in the Berkshires who diagnosed her with a urinary tract infection, gave us antibiotics, and told us to go home. I was angry at the stroke and vestibular ear diagnosis that appeared to be discounted once Sandy was re-tested at The Hospital. I was angry that for 40 days from the onset of the disease to the end, Sandy had to suffer – along with me, my family, and a circle of very loving friends.

I was angry at a hospital system that can, at times, be so cold. For example, when Sandy had to be moved from one floor to another to have a procedure, and then transferred again after the procedure was completed, the night nurse was concerned that the room had to be cleared immediately upon Sandy's departure. She ordered me to take all of the many flowers that Sandy had received and bring them home because there was no place to store them. "If you leave them here," she told me, "I'll throw them out."

Faced with a flower crisis before Sandy's surgery, I asked, "Why can't I just take them to the other floor, instead?" The night nurse replied, "She doesn't have a room on that floor yet. There is nowhere to put them." At this point, I knew I didn't want to be a flower schlepper and said, "I understand it is my responsibility." Always the problem solver, I decided to go to the other floor and ask a nurse if I could store the flowers there until my wife arrived. The nurse said no problem and gave me a locker in an empty room, which was a simple kindness that the other nurse had been incapable of giving. I thought of the BLT scene in *Five Easy Pieces* but knew the reference would be lost on her. In my mind, what wasn't lost was the larger picture of The Hospital's bureaucratic structure. For what they are billing, maybe they should throw in some dedicated flower schleppers.

If I hold on to these anger straws, I know they won't support me. They will distance me from my daughter, whom I love more than anything. They will strangulate the relationships I have with my family. And eventually they will destroy the relationships I have with many caring friends who only want the best for me. The anger would simply fester and not let me accept Sandy's death and the wonderful life we had together. That life and love are too important to me to let them wither. Family and friends are what matter most to me.

With a little perspective, I have come to understand that there are no villains in this piece. Dr. Frankfurter, a brilliant diagnostician, wanted to help in every way he could. Quality of life had a different meaning for him than it did for me. Coincidently, I discovered that his daughter was undergoing plasmapheresis on the eighth floor to combat multiple sclerosis, and treatments were helping her.

Dr. Kaiser, an MS and autoimmune specialist who covered for Dr. Frankfurter during the Fourth of July weekend, came to visit Sandy and me in The Hospice. Dr. Kaiser said he had told his wife of my decision not to allow a feeding tube to prolong Sandy's debilitated quality of life and admired me for acting in my wife's best interests. Many of the residents, including Dr. Tao and Dr. Faisel, came to say goodbye. When I was leaving for The Hospice, the nurses on the eighth floor commented about how I stuck by my wife and was there all the time for her. Previously, I had prayed with them. I am an atheist, but I recognized that when people reach out to comfort you, you should take their hand. The warmth that they felt for my wife and me was truly touching.

The health aides, who gently swabbed her mouth or gave her a spa treatment to make her feel better, were gentle and caring. Mrs. Jaipore, a case manager who records procedures for billing, emerged from behind her computer when she saw me sobbing. She knew I was in pain and took the time to comfort me. She was of the Jain religion, which holds that all life is sacred. Sandy and I had previously seen Jain temples in India and had visited a Jain family. Throughout our days at the hospital, when I needed to feel Mrs. Jaipore's kindness, she and I would often speak about Sandy.

There were others. If I had a problem, the nurse managers, Tova and Ms. Gibbons, in thoracic and neurology, respectively, would acknowledge it and intervene to correct it as soon as possible. They knew the patient came first. Both Dr. Fox, a thoracic surgeon and colleague of Dr. Torres, and Dr. Erush, an oncologist, had sustained and friendly conversations with me about Sandy's condition. They told me my ideas were thoughtful, reasoned, and based on both medical knowledge and my wife's wishes, thus enabling me to focus my thinking. Meanwhile, the Palliative Care Team would listen intently as I recapped my experiences in advocating for my wife and then would present my position to the Neurology Team. And Dr. Kenneth, our internist, visited Sandy each weekday morning to see how she was doing. He wanted her to be well.

So at The Hospital, there was a great sense of humanity – and inhumanity. In the grieving process, I have to learn what and what not to accept. The more I can accept – the more I can recognize where my tears originate – the better off I'll be. I want Sandy's life, not her death, to be commemorated. The only reason I let this part of the story be so raw and unvarnished is that Sandy is still teaching me to become a whole person. She never took Meredith to Disneyland, even though Meredith and I would have gone in a heartbeat. She felt it was artificial and painted a rosy fantasy of the real world. Sandy was more interested in exploring the real world without the pabulum. Sometimes one needs Disneyland, and sometimes one needs to see the world without the rose-colored glasses. Disneyland, while enjoyable, really doesn't make you stronger; knowing clearly what life offers does. Sandy would want Charlie and Dexter to be as strong as she was (and, I would add, as beautiful).

When you lose half of yourself, there is a vacuum. And in your rush to fill up that empty space, you have no idea whether you're really filling it in a way that ultimately will make you feel whole again. So my only thought was to proceed slowly. For example, after Sandy died, I couldn't deal with all her clothes in the closet and dresser. Meredith and her good friend – who is also named Meredith – came to pack up and donate Sandy's clothes. Everything went – except for a Max Mara suit that

Sandy had bought in Italy and that her friend, Alice, wanted to save for Charlie. And a tribal jacket I was going to give away to another friend. When I touched the jacket, it was like remembering the taste of chocolate – an indulgence, rich and sweet, to be slowly savored.

On one of our trips that focused on ethnic minorities in China, Sandy and I visited Yunnan province, which is reputedly where the mythical state of Shangri-La is located. Shangri-La, as Charlie and Dexter will know, is an earthly paradise described in the 1933 novel *Lost Horizon*. Yunnan's landscape, with its sunshine, mountains, rolling valleys, and crystal clear air, surrounded by fluffy clouds, looks like heaven on earth. There, in a shop within a museum, I saw a wondrously beautiful Yao's woman's jacket. I had Sandy try it on, with its circular patterned black and light grey tie-dyed fabric, with small wisps of beaded embroidery, round silver metal buttons, pleated details and delicate stitching. Wearing it, she lit up Shangri-La. In my vivid memory of that day, I can still see her smile. And to think I almost gave it away. She wore the jacket with some simple black pants to many a happy occasion.

Now the jacket is being framed in a shadow box to preserve it and will hang over the fireplace in my home. If I rushed through the process, as I originally intended, I would not have been able to spend all the time I needed with the jacket and its memories. To move forward, you sometimes have to look back. There is no rush. Just put one foot in front of the other and see what each day brings. If you need to step into the past to feel or understand something, go there. It will help with the pacing. Try to want less and stay in the moment. If I can follow this guidance, it should help me heal. It should help all of us heal.

Everyone experiences loss. Everyone experiences grieving. Many of my friends who call to comfort me relate the stories of their own loss and bereavement. They cry as if it happened yesterday. The pain is real. My friend Phil, who lost his first wife, Lanni, early in life, told me an interesting story when he learned I was going to put together a book for Charlie and Dexter about Sandy's legacy. He reminded me that when a neighbor, Olivia, died, her husband, Jack, who loved her very much, spent the next eight years putting picture books together, like *Olivia on Vacation, Olivia Cooking,* and *Olivia Gardening.* He would hand them out at family celebrations. "You are not going to become like Jack," Phil said. "Are you?"

Many of my friends have called to check on me. The question I'd be asked most often and have not known how to answer until recently, is, "Are you OK?" Finally, I figured out an answer. I reply, "I am as OK as I can be." I like that answer. It is everything and nothing all at once.

6. A Memory

MEMORIES ARE A POWERFUL FORCE and we must not forget what our eyes have seen. It is also a creative process. Each time we remember something we subtly change it. I know these things to be true because Barbara Weinstein, the officiant at Sandy's funeral, listened to a speaker at the Park Avenue Synagogue and summarized the lecture for me. I often tease her that her membership in the synagogue gives her an immediate connection to anything one would ever need in New York. I wanted to say her connection gets her those goods and services below retail ~~force~~ but thought better of it. *price* Sometimes my dry humor does not translate well and, for sure, this was one of those times. Sandy used to know how to edit me; now I have to figure it out for myself. Barbara's distillation continued. Memories are malleable. We reinvent our narrative. Memories confer morality.

At no time were Barbara's insights on memory clearer to me than at a dinner I had with Jeanette at a pretty mediocre French bistro in the Berkshires. After a drink, we reflected on Sandy and our grieving process. Funny, in the aftermath of Sandy's death, unvarnished feelings rise to the surface when you are with friends.

Sandy was the first contemporary in our circle of friends to die, and as a result, we all felt vulnerable. Friends thought about their own relationships and asked themselves, "What would I do if I were in Larry's situation?" Unfortunately, since I was in Larry's situation, I sometimes responded that I had done nothing heroic. I just tried to care for her the best I could.

Jeanette, whose upbringing compels her to take care of people she cares about, knows how to reach the substance of things quickly. I heard through the Indian Lake grapevine that some of the women Jeanette plays tennis with were trying to set me up. Just what I needed – the brisket brigade.

Dryly I said, "Jeanette, you know I am never going to have sex again." She responded without blinking. "It's only been a couple of weeks. You are not ready." I felt she would protect me and maybe in a year I'd see where I am. I felt safe.

Then Jeanette unintentionally shattered my safety by asking, "Larry, in your talks with Sandy in the hospital, did she give you permission to live? To be with another woman?" I started to cry. It was a weeping cry with tears that, at first, I could control. But as the memory deepened, more tears started to flow. Minutes passed before I managed to verbalize my feelings. I remembered a conversation with Sandy that I hadn't previously documented. I had tried to document everything I could, just to keep my sanity, but Jeanette's questions reminded me that this particular memory had escaped.

When she was close to the end but still conscious, Sandy told me, "I know you will find another woman." I thought she was at the stage in the disease where her personality was changing, and she was telling me this because she did not want me to

move on. She wanted to be with me. "No," Jeanette said, "she's telling you that because she loves you and, even in death, wants to make sure you're taken care of. That is what people who love each other do." I paused to absorb the thought.
Could it be that Jeanette was right, and that my reaction was that I was not accepting the fact that Sandy was leaving me? Was Sandy the one who was in control, and was I the one reeling into space? Or were we both lost?

If Barbara is right and memories are malleable, I will have to reinvent my narrative as I continue. I need to know what I can and should do. My therapist, who is very on target, told me, "In grief counseling, there are no 'shoulds' in this process." I understand. Put one foot in front of the other, take one day at a time, live in the present, go slowly, and so on.

On the other hand, there are "shoulds" in the past that selective memories reveal. What should I do when I feel lonely? Should I learn from the loneliness and treat it as if it were a traveling companion? How I remember my wife and our simple, loving relationship will in large part tell me where I should be going. Some people in this process never get out of the past. They become stuck, unable to move forward. I know of a very lovely person who, after her husband died, did not want the closets emptied of his clothes. It is four years later, and the clothes are still in the closets. I understand her; if his clothes are there, he is, too. It takes courage to move forward.

I do want to move forward. At this point I am just not sure how to do it. I do know the writing helps. The keyboard on my laptop is waterproofed, tested by my tears. The catharsis makes me feel better as my days progress. I feel, at times, a lightness of being, and those times are good. Other times, it is not so good, and not even some magical thinking can make me feel better. Someone once described life as a balancing act. To be successful at it you need equilibrium. This book is a toast to all of us who are learning to walk again.

7. Practicum

THERE IS THIS OLD JOKE. A Jew reads that the polar ice caps are melting. He goes to the rabbi and says, "Global warming is here. The ice caps are melting." He pauses, thinks for a minute and then says, "So rabbi, what does this mean for the Jews as a people?" Global warming affects all people's lives, unless you have an ostrich personality that ignores scientific fact by burying your head underground. It defies logic, but some argue the view is nicer if you don't see anything.

In the joke, the Jew needs the rabbi to put things in context so he can discern how to practically make sense of the impending disaster. It is the same with Sandy's end-of-life experience. People die once, and therefore they are novices about the end-of-life process. Most people won't die as quickly as Sandy did but will suffer with a prolonged illness. We all battle death and eventually it will win. But during the process, do we see clearly — or are we like ostriches? What practical meaning did Sandy's life have in our struggle? I discovered this meaning in a simple and beautiful email that my niece, Jennifer, sent to me on my birthday:

Dear Larry,

I would love to wish you a Happy Birthday, but I feel it may not be so. I guess this will be a tough day for you. I am glad that Meredith and her family are with you. I hope you are surrounded by good friends as well. I will wish you the ability to go on and live the life that Sandy and you built together. I can't believe she would want you to stop doing that. You have a loving group of friends and family that will be there for you when you are ready to go forward.

At Sandy's memorial service, as I was listening to all her friends speak about her, I understood on a new level what I have always known in my heart. Sandy was an extraordinary woman. Over the years, when I spoke with her, she always listened intently and spoke to me in such a way that I felt important and bright and loved by her.

What I learned in listening to her friends is that the recurrent theme of Sandy's life is that she made everyone feel that way. That is a special gift to possess, and I am grateful to have learned so much about her. I feel like I can take some of what I learned about her and improve myself and my life, and teach my children that listening to others and showing compassion can only bring joy – not only to yourself, but to those around you.

Your Loving Niece,

Jennifer

Jennifer, a nurse, expressed Sandy's legacy in terms of her own life. So if Jennifer can do it, why can't others in the medical establishment do it, too? If vestiges of that community can't, for whatever reason, is it not up to all of us to speak with a clear voice so they will have to do the right thing? Who would argue that the medical community should do less? The National Right to Life Committee, a "pro-life" organization that was established in the late 1960s, would have politicians and doctors intervene if someone is denied lifesaving medical treatment, food, and fluids.

The group's thinking is that the default position should be to prolong life and that, therefore, roadblocks need to be in place to stop people from exercising their right to die with dignity. (See www.nrlc.org/archive/MedEthics/index.html.)

In a *New York Times* article, "Coverage for End-of-Life Talks Gaining Ground" (Aug. 30, 2014), Pam Belluck reports that Medicare does not have reimbursement codes to pay health-care providers to help patients complete advance directives. Although some private insurance companies are paying health-care providers up to $250 for end-of-life conversations, most elderly patients have only Medicare, with no secondary insurance coverage. "Reimbursement rates for talking are much lower than for medical procedures," Ms. Belluck writes. "But doctors say without compensation, there is pressure to keep appointments short to squeeze in more patients."

The United States has the most expensive health-care system in the world. Some might argue, therefore, that we have created one of the best health-care systems in the world. Those people would be wrong. The Commonwealth Fund ranks international health-care systems on the basis of quality, access, efficiency, equity, and healthy lives. In 2014, out of 11 industrialized nations that were studied, the United States ranks dead last. (See www.commonwealthfund.org/publications/fund-reports/2014/jun/mirror-mirror.) In part, the dysfunction of our health-care system lies in a smokescreen of "higher morality" that gives shelter to people who do not want end-of-life conversations to be the norm. Such people prey on fears. They think Americans will be afraid that government will sneak into their bedrooms and snuff out their freedom of choice while they sleep.

Political leaders who employ this rhetoric develop shills who move the crowd into the carnival tent while picking their pockets all at the same time. Religious fundamentalism intertwining with right-to-life ideologues often prolong a painful death. If you can see Russia from your kitchen window, you can also envision "death panels" run by faceless bureaucrats rallying a base that is afraid of government invading their freedom to choose.

Moral outrage that Obamacare is gutting health care in America with no valid alternative is another sleight-of-hand argument to misdirect people to follow a particular political agenda. It appeals to people who enjoy posing in the ostrich position. To these people, I would argue the Lockean principle, so embedded in our Founding Fathers' philosophy. My freedom ends where your nose begins. So keep your nose out of my right to determine humane end-of-life decisions for my wife, and I will keep my nose out of your decision to prolong the life of your wife for as long as you wish.

In whose interest was it that Sandy be kept alive when it was clear that her family knew there no longer was a viable quality of life? In whose interest was it that the doctors could ignore her living will by not having it scanned into their electronic record-keeping system and letting it languish in her looseleaf binder? How could her doctors make intelligent and compassionate choices without following Sandy's living will? Why didn't her doctors use her living will as an advance directive and include it within their medical orders – so that all health-care providers would have been legally obligated to follow her wishes?

To answer those questions, ask a more essential one: Who benefits? Is it the patient or the health-care providers? Consider the widely reported fact that, by far, the largest portion of total medical costs in the United States is consumed by patients in the last year of life. The hospitals, doctors, and HMOs know how to be reimbursed for their services. It is more than a cottage industry. Look at the number of people employed in the medical billing profession. End-of-life treatments are a judgment call – a very profitable judgment call. The more tests you run, the more procedures you do, the better the bottom line. Vested medical interests have learned to make a living off the government's teat, flowing with taxpayer dollars, while expounding the virtues of free enterprise and capitalism.

Doctors who see their role as aggressively intervening to save lives will always find one more treatment until the pipeline runs dry. They will keep hope alive that the illness can be cured or at least controlled with an acceptable quality of life. To them an end-of-life conversation means, "When should I pass the patient off to the hospice?"

But true end-of-life conversations are so much more than handing off the patient to Palliative Care. The view of Dr. Atul

Gawande, author of *Being Mortal,* is described atop an article he wrote for *The New Yorker* a few years ago: Modern medicine is "good at staving off death with aggressive interventions – and bad at knowing when to focus, instead, on improving the days a terminal patent has left." So the "hard question," Dr. Gawande writes, "is not how we can afford this system's expense. It is how we can build a health-care system that will actually help dying patients achieve what's most important to them at the end of their lives." (See www.newyorker.com/magazine/2010/08/02/letting-go-2.)

In "The Town Where Everyone Talks About Death" on National Public Radio (Morning Edition, March 5, 2014), Chana Joffe-Walt looks at La Crosse, Wisc., where 96 percent of the people have an advance directive, living will, or something similar, compared with 30 percent nationwide. According to *The Dartmouth Atlas of Health Care,* which documented Medicare costs in 2009 around the country, shows that patients at La Crosse's Gundersen medical center spend an average of 13.5 days of their final two years of life at an average cost of $18,000. It's 31 days and $59,000 at UCLA's medical centers; 39 days and $64,000 at the University of Miami, $66,000, and 54 days at New York University's Langone Medical Center. In one New York Hospital, the cost reportedly is as high as $75,000.

In La Crosse, people have the necessary conversations about life and death. It turns out that if people understand ahead of time what they may face with the hospital-induced "white-coat syndrome," they can make informed, intelligent end-of-life decisions. They can say, "If this happens, stop treatment." In

La Crosse, the emphasis is on what the patient wants, what he or she sees as reasonable treatment after discussions with family members and medical professionals. They answer questions like, "Do you want a feeding tube if you can't eat on your own?" In many other parts of the country, it's what the medical establishment wants, with just enough consultation to give the impression that it's doing what is best for the patient.

In La Crosse, there also is peer pressure for families and neighbors to take time to have the hard conversations they may need before completing an advance directive. In many other parts of the country, conversations about death may occur about as often as some children talk with their parents about sex; that is, not very often at all. In La Crosse, patients are empowered to make important decisions affecting their lives. Elsewhere, such empowerment is not shared at all, or it is shared only somewhat when it is convenient for the powers that be. In La Crosse, there is an established network of health-care workers who are trained to guide people through the hard conversations. But elsewhere, for the most part, such networks are just starting to develop.

In a "Coping with Cancer" study cited by Dr. Gawande in his *New Yorker* article, two-thirds of terminally ill cancer patients reported that they'd had "no discussion with their doctors about their goals for end-of-life care – despite being, on average, just four months from death." But the third of the patients who did have end-of-life discussions "suffered less, were physically more capable, and were better able, for a longer period, to interact with others." In addition, Dr. Gawande noted, "six months after the patients died their family members were much less likely to experience persistent major depression."

One of my friends, Dr. Steve Tarnoff, told me that he and his wife, Ann – each of whom had previously lost a spouse and subsequently found each other – went online to fill out an advance directive known as "Five Wishes." (See www.agingwithdignity.org/five-wishes.php.) The document enables you to make clear: (1) Who you want to make health-care decisions for you when you can't make them; (2) the kind of medical treatment you want or don't want; (3) how comfortable you want to be; (4) how you want people to treat you, and (5) what you want your loved ones to know. Once finalized, those choices become a basis for conversation when you enter a hospital.

Several states, including New York and Massachusetts, have developed programs known as MOLST (Medical Orders for Life-Sustaining Treatment). Unlike health-care proxies and advance directives, MOLST documents represent your doctor's orders and become part of your medical record. There are bright pink MOLST forms that one can download.

A similar program called POLST (Physician Orders for Life-Sustaining Treatment) has matured in at least two states, Oregon and West Virginia, and has been endorsed by California, Colorado, Georgia, Hawaii, Idaho, Louisiana, Montana, New York, North Carolina, Pennsylvania, Tennessee, Utah, and Washington State. More and more people, in more and more states, are coming to realize that end-of-life conversations are essential for meaningful, dignified care for patients and their families. And instead of one end-of-life conversation, people should have a series of advance-directive conversations. Indeed, as suggested in a recent committee report from the nonprofit Institute of Medicine, an independent arm of the National Academy of Sciences, such conversations can include "seriously ill children and adolescents, who may be able to participate in end-of-life decision making on their own behalf."

Calling for a sweeping overhaul of end-of-life care, the report seeks to make palliative care an extensive part of every doctor's medical education, and it recommends that Medicare, Medicaid, and private insurance companies provide reimbursements to promote decent, comprehensive, and humane end-of-life interventions. (For information about the report, including a link for downloading a free PDF version, see www.nap.edu/catalog/18748/dying-in-america-improving-quality-and-honoring-individual-preferences-near.)

In a *New York Times* article that references the report, Nina Bernstein underscores one of its key points: "For most people, death does not come suddenly. ... With 48 times as many people reaching 85 than a century ago, and triple the number who turn 65, the likely course of death is long and unpredictable."

But as Ms. Bernstein points out in paraphrasing one of the report's authors, Dr. Joan M. Teno, a leading gerontologist and professor at Brown University: "The system was never engineered to support families through this, and its financial incentives reward harmful transitions among homes, hospitals, and nursing homes."

"It's all about profit margins," says Dr. Teno. "It is not about caring for people." Adds Dr. Jack Resnick, another specialist in the field: "The way the reimbursement system works, these decisions are not made on the basis of what the individuals need. They're based on what the institutions need." (See www.nytimes.com/2014/09/26/nyregion/family-fights-health-care-system-for-simple-request-to-die-at-home.html.)

If Congress and our political system can ever bring themselves to support individuals over financial institutions, the palliative-care initiatives that we so desperately need – along with comprehensive legislation to reform our dysfunctional health-care system – might actually come about. But wind blowing from opposite directions, not to mention a Congressional approval rating under 10 percent, does little but create inertia.

Gerrymandered districts and vested lobbying groups are content with the status quo. The question is: As more and more Americans are living and dying with the present system, are we content? I know from my own experience with end-of-life care that to stymie change and suppress human dignity is not acceptable.

And I know I am not alone. I know there are many people who want to shine a light on those in private enterprise and government who put profits ahead of a person's right to die with dignity. In Nina Bernstein's article, Dr. Joanne Lynn, a hospice physician and end-of-life policy expert, points to federal budget cuts for seniors' meals and asks, "Why can I get a $100,000 drug but I can't get supper?"

The system measures the value of life in years spent, not in the quality of life one is living. One way to correct this flaw is to compel doctors to put advance directives signed by patients into the medical orders for all cases, not just cases where the patient is critically ill. All medical providers should be obligated both legally and morally to honor the patient's choices. The way the law is currently structured makes it difficult to complete the MOLST in a timely fashion. So what happens if the patient cannot complete the MOLST in time? The default position currently allows the medical establishment to prolong life with artificial electronic gizmos and untried treatments. It ignores the patient's wishes to simply stop trying.

Where Sandy was being treated, the turning point came when she stopped trying. She was in a world-class teaching hospital, and many people there did treat her well. But some staff people are oblivious to the impact of their actions. For example, the coordinator of physical therapy denied Sandy access to the one thoracic walker she needed to exercise once she was transferred to the neurology wing. "We can't move the walker up two floors for a physical therapy session," the coordinator said. "It just is too difficult. We'll have two people hold her as she tries to walk."

The walker never came – and Sandy, beaten down by the system, never walked again. Even earlier, when Sandy was in danger of falling and had difficulty walking without support, the chief technician during a PET scan seemed incapable of treating her with dignity. I was told she needed some radioactive dye, and I should come back in an hour while she stayed in a room watching television. Forty minutes later, as I was returning in the hall, I heard Sandy calling me. I rushed around the corridor and grabbed her. She told me she had gone out of the room several times and had to go to the bathroom. I took her, got a wheelchair, and asked to speak to the head of the department.

A young man came and I showed him Sandy's "fall risk" bracelet. "This bracelet means a patient should not be walking alone," I said. "She could have fallen and broken a hip. Why wasn't someone there to help her?" "I know. I am sorry," he said, acknowledging that it should not have happened. Then, for my troubles, he offered me a $5 Starbucks gift card. I looked at him incredulously and refused his offer. What is troubling is that I saw the humor in his stupidity, and he did not.

Listening to my stories, my doctor friend Steve Tarnoff asked me why hadn't I reported the incidents to the committee overseeing such matters at The Hospital. That committee, he said, can change the way things happen. I responded, "How was I to know such a committee exists?" As a result, I started to ask myself what exactly was being taught at The Hospital, and what is happening in other hospitals that may be lower on the food chain?

In palliative care, everyone is trained to realize the impact of their actions. Palliative care is medical care focused on the prevention and relief of suffering, and on supporting the best possible quality of life for patients and their families regardless of the stages of a disease. That was the blessed pain management Sandy received at The Hospice.

According to the palliative-care section of The Hospital's website, "the focus of a hospice relies on the belief that each of us has the right to die pain-free and with dignity and that our loved ones will receive support." Sandy experienced comfort, and there was a willingness to do anything for her and her family to help. She was treated with dignity and everyone was on the same page. No faceless bureaucrats here; just a medical team working in unison to ensure that the patient and the family comes first. Everyone – whether a doctor, nurse, orderly, social worker, or massage therapist – was willing to schlep flowers.

In the words of Dr. Stephanie Pincus, a neighbor of mine who helped organize the committee that produced the Institute of Medicine's report, "The fact that many physicians have not been trained in how to take care of dying patients other than by 'doing things to them' is a great failing in our educational system for medical professionals."

In order to move on, I need to see things in a way that helps people.

In my life with Sandy, I always did. She was my partner, and she had the same vision. Holding up a mirror to some of the practices that ignore patient empowerment will enable certain medical providers to see their reflections clearly and apply the necessary remedies. As of now, the default position is to prolong life. That is simply wrong. The default position must be to honor a patient's choice in an advance directive that is included in the medical orders.

In writing this book, I want Sandy's legacy to rest in a safe place – not only with Charlie and Dexter, but with everyone who reads these pages and knows the emptiness that loss brings. With loss, however, also comes empathy for others, and a bonding with all who have experienced the death of a loved one. We simply have to treat our loved ones, at the end of their lives, better than we presently do. Sandy's beautiful life and tragic death are a testament to that mission.

8. A Question of Change

WE LIVE IN A POLITICAL CULTURE that is expert at changing the meanings of words to foster political goals. For example, employers become "job creators," permitting rich people to control power becomes "limited government," and —best of all — anti-abortionists become "right-to-life advocates." Everyone in America has his or her right to life guaranteed in the Declaration of Independence. Unfortunately the Declaration has no legal standing, although it does embody what American ethics should be.

But the right to life by no means bestows a right to prolong life whenever and wherever possible. It is a right to live your life with quality and to end your life with dignity and minimal pain. Prophylactic suicide is the antidote to preachings of a right to prolong life at any cost, an approach that benefits the nation's extended medical establishment. If the reasoning behind prophylactic suicide were institutionalized, many of the outrageous end-of-life problems that people face would dissolve. Caregivers would be free from the legal and procedural battles that currently muck up the system. It is a simple solution that can strip away many of the prickly thorns that currently surround end-of-life.

Why not campaign for that — unless, of course, the opposition succeeds in demonizing advocates and producing a media feeding frenzy? Dr. Jack Kevorkian, who advocated for euthanasia from the 1970s to the 1990s, was prosecuted, and his ideas were unfairly ridiculed. That's because many Americans may have an unrealistic fear of dying. In fact, many comedians understand that reality, and they know we need a release from our fear.

The media, meanwile, often trivialize the subject with coverage a mile wide and an inch deep. In an obituary of Kevorkian, Michigan journalist Jack Lessenberry notes that the doctor exposed American taboos by recognizing "the elephant in the room." Many people would opt for death if their lives were not worth living. (See Keith Schneider in *The New York Times,* June 3, 2011).

A doctor confided to me that people can end their lives today simply by taking a combination of over-the-counter drugs available at any neighborhood pharmacy. Of course, she did not want to reveal the specifics, so one is not sure whether to look in the cold-remedy aisle or the toothpaste display. I wondered whether one could earn Rite Aid points on such a purchase. The conversation is still *sub rosa.*

Baby boomers are now approaching the grey age where it is no longer smart to marginalize the end-of-life conversation. We need to shed light on the issue no matter where it may lead us. Of course, some people make a living at marginalizing very sane and humane ideas. The question is, should we let them? I am always wary of people who say they have the right answer. I believe that the right question is more important. For me, prophylactic suicide is more of a question than an answer. What if we embraced prophylactic suicide? What else would have to change? Would it make us a better society? As Judith Wizowaty of Burlington, Vt., wrote in a *New York Times* "Sunday Dialogue" contribution (Nov. 16, 2014): "How absurd that those of us who have made our own decisions for over 80 years should be denied their last choice – the right to decide the time of our own last rite."

In the same dialogue, Vance Weaver of New York contemplates his own death: "Will I just keel over unexpectedly one morning (fine!), or will I get some miserably debilitating affliction (cancer, perhaps, or kidney failure) and have to go through a nightmare of 'the latest' treatments before the doctors let me go, or will I need to make my way to a bridge or a high window when I decide that I have lived long enough? It would be nice to have a lethal, painless and legal pill on my dresser…."

Clearly people should have a right to prophylactic suicide, but it needs to be regulated to avoid abuse by family members, caregivers, business associates, and lawyers (although it is hard to imagine the latter as being opportunistic). David Johnson of Greenwood, Colo., says in *The New York Times* that someone wishing to die could "obtain a determination by two disinterested persons that the desire is based upon rational reasons." A doctor could then fulfill the patient's wishes without fear of legal prosecution. Insurance companies, HMOs, and other parties should not be permitted to structure economic disincentives to prevent a patient's final rational decision.

In the Netherlands, if you are at the end of your life and do not want it to contninue, two doctors can codify your wishes and your primary-care physician can prescribe suicide pills. You can choose to die at home, surrounded by people and things you cherish. The pills, which have a bitter taste, can be mixed with jam and then given to the patient. Actually, it's an elegant process. But in most of the United States, you are going to be on life support, with tubes protruding from your weakened body, and beseiged by a sterile hospital atmosphere. We value *life* support when we should be valuing *quality-of-life* support. Our country lives in fear that institutions will be sued if they make the wrong choice. Yet places like the Netherlands and Denmark have very high happiness indexes when compared to the United States. Unlike us, these nations know how to construct institutions that honor people's choices.

In America, we like to think that individual choice is paramount in preserving freedom. So why is a rational choice to end life so stigmatized? Physician-assisted suicide continues to be prohibited in most states. Exceptions include Oregon, Vermont, and Washington, which allow it by state law. It also is permitted under court rulings in Montana and New Mexico's Bernalillo County. Everywhere else it can be tantamount to murder. But we must learn how to distinguish between murder and mercy – and to act accordingly. Otherwise, *The Grievance* will continue without relief.

Epilogue

As I WRITE THIS, it is about six months since Sandy's funeral. I feel I have put in the work necessary to be able to move on and enjoy laughter again. I said goodbye with a hug for my wonderful therapist, Mary Kay King, who knew exactly how to listen to me and help me process my feelings. I also did group therapy as a transition to meet other people who were experiencing the loss of a partner.

During that time, I learned that men who lose their spouses generally take about three months to start considering a new relationship, while women who are widowed take more than a year.

It seems that women tend to have more intricate relationships with people and do most of the social networking in the marriage. So when a man loses his spouse, and recognizes that he has been inept at building a network that could comfort him, he sees that he needs to reach out to someone who can provide such a service. Another factor is that women tend to outlive men, and the numbers therefore favor a man's finding someone compatible earlier. So the generalities say I am ready to go forward.

And yet, when Barbara Weinstein emailed me a newspaper article that she thought I'd find interesting, my memories intensified. In "Hoping for a Good Death" *(The New York Times, Dec. 2, 2014)*, Elizabeth Reis, chair of the Women's and

Gender Studies department at the University of Oregon, illustrates how the medical establishment's default position is to prolong life – even if the patient and the family do not want that.

Dr. Reis's 78-year-old father specifically said he did not want machines to keep him alive if he had "any physical or mental incapacities." Her father did not have an advance directive, and he had a heart attack in a restaurant. After he was revived by EMTs, doctors in the hospital froze his brain to decrease the risk of brain injury and hooked him up to a ventilator, a feeding tube, and various other electronic devices. On the fourth day, the family was informed that "the big picture was terrible." The family decided to remove the machines, and Dr. Reis's father died on the fifth day.

One Oregon medical resident even told the family, "I don't think you gave him enough of a chance." The arrogance of a physician who does not know a patient or the family to presume that he knows what should be done is staggering. True, this patient did not have a living will, but the game apparently is to make a family acquiesce in letting things take their course and then hope for the best. It's also true that the patient did receive a high level of medical care. Doctors were trying to save a life as they had been trained to do. But the question is: What type of emotional care was given to the family in this situation when it was clear that the patient had expressed his wishes orally, though not in writing?

Dr. Reis recognizes that doctors are hesitant to immediately talk to families about their loved one's approaching death, that "no one wants to dash hopes for recovery." She concludes that "confronting the end from the beginning" is "giving loved ones an opportunity to … stretch hope in a way that accommodates a better death."

Sandy did have a living will but received the same arrogant treatment when Dr. Frankfurter told me, "I know when to call it, and this is not the time." He was playing the same game that the Oregon doctor had played. The point is that living wills can lessen feelings of guilt when a family has to make end-of-life judgments. With such documents, families have the right to honor their loved one's choices and combat arrogance. Without them, a medical abyss awaits.

On reading a first draft of this epilogue, Barbara wrote to me: "I like what you wrote, but your pain comes through your comments … not sure you want it to." I explained: "The only way I know to deal with pain is to let it out so I can move on." Mary Kay King said I would have relapses, and if any of them are persistent, she will always be there for me. The flash remembrances that are triggered by an article or place or conversation are the normal part of the healing process.

My daughter and I now regularly meet for dinner – alone, so our conversation will not be interrupted. Four months after Sandy's passing, Meredith exhibited a kind of magical thinking. "I can't believe she is dead," she said suddenly. "I think of her as still alive. There is no reason she should be dead."

I knew exactly what she meant. We'd been given hope and we were still clinging to that hope, even after we had made the hard decision to advocate for Sandy's end of life. For us, it was the best decision we could have made, and it happened in an instant, frozen in time. If we had not made it when we did, the consequences would have been unbearable for Sandy. People told us, "You gave her a gift." They were right. We did not let anyone harm her by giving her a life she would not want to lead. We stayed strong and pushed back against the medical system. After all, isn't "first, do no harm" a time-honored tenet of medical practice? For me, the issue is no longer only what happened to Sandy; it's a wish I have for all people in America. You and your family should have the right to die without being harmed. People should have a good life – and a good death.

At my dinners with Meredith, which we've been having about every two weeks since Sandy's death, she has shown incredible strength. "If I can live through what happened with Mommy's dying," she told me, "I know now I can live through anything." Charlie, now eight years old, is the same way. She comforts me with her radiance. I recently took her to the Museum of Modern Art to see Matisse's *Cut-Outs*. We took a two-hour class together where we collaboratively made our own big cut-out in the style of Matisse. Dexter, now three, has discovered trucks. He can name each one on a construction site and has learned to kick a soccer ball so it goes whooshing by me.

At dinner I tell Meredith I am thinking of dating again. Even though I still have an interesting life in New York City, I need a relationship. I know it will not replace the one I had but will be something new. Meredith is happy for me. She smiles, and says, "Do we have to have a conversation about safe sex?" We laugh and talk about my upcoming trip to Antarctica and how I am looking forward to it. My cousin Marcy, who lives in Tel Aviv, emailed me saying, "I can't possibly see why anyone would go to Antarctica. Is it for the penguins? I replied by return email, "No ... for the solitude." In reality, it is to mark a new phase in my life where I will try to reach out and meet new people. It is for the companionship. Meredith and I continue to talk and sip a really nice Malbec in the wine bar when, and all of a sudden, I see tears welling up in her eyes. "What is it?" I ask. "I can't help it," she says. "I miss Mommy so much." I take her hand and say, "I know. I do, too," as my tears start to follow hers. Then we start to laugh together. "I guess I now have to be both a father and a mother to you." Suddenly, in my mind's eye, I see a scene from *Fiddler on the Roof* where the cast is singing "Sunrise, Sunset." I think of my own happiness and tears over the past six months and I know how fortunate I am to be here now.

Surfing End-of-Life

FOR PEOPLE WHO WISH to avoid well-engineered end-of-life traps, the key lies in understanding the system and recognizing that laws vary from state to state about what it takes to execute an acceptable advance directive. The following online resources, presented in no particular order, may be helpful.

~

www.mountsinai.org/patient-care/service-areas/palliative-care
Here are details about the philosophy and services of New York City's Mount Sinai Hospital, as well the inpatient and outpatient programs of its palliative-care unit.

www.honoringchoicesmass.com
This is a Massachusetts initiative that honors advance directives in health-care planning. The website includes issues in advance planning, the planning itself, and supportive community resources.

www.honoringchoices.org
Minnesota's Honoring Choices website provides video stories, documentaries, and other material to help engage families in end-of-life conversations.

www.compassionandchoice.org
Check this site for consultation and other resources, including a state-by-state guide for advance directives, from an organization "committed to helping everyone have the best death possible."

www.health.ny.gov/professionals/patients/patient_rights/molst
This website describes New York State's program for people who

might die within a year and explores the use of Medical Orders for Life-Sustaining Treatments (MOLST) to insure that advance planning will have legal support and be honored by health-care providers.

www.agingwithdignity.org/five-wishes.php
This site contains comprehensive information, including downloads, about the *Five Wishes* living will.

www.polst.org
Learn about End-Of-Life planning in various states where seriously ill and frail patients can choose treatments they want – or do not want.

www.compassionandsupport.org
End-of-life directives and palliative-care services from a leading organization serving western and central New York State are described.

www.nap.edu/catalog/18748/dying-in-america-improving-quality-and-honoring-individual-preferences-near
You can download a PDF version here of the Institute of Medicine's comprehensive report on "Dying in America."

www.theconversationproject.org
This site includes a "starter kit" from a group whose slogan is, "When it comes to end-of-life care, one conversation can make all the difference."

www.deathwithdignity.org
Check this overview of Oregon, Vermont, and Washington laws that support physician-assisted suicide.

www.nhdd.org/public-resources
The National Health Care Decisions Day is building a network to support advance planning.

www.gundersenhealth.org/respecting-choices
The La Crosse, Wisc., community's end-of-life program, begun more than 20 years ago, emphasizes "high-quality care" with lower costs.

www.thectac.org

The Coalition to Transform Advanced Care seeks to "transform advanced illness care by empowering consumers, changing the health-care delivery system, improving public and private policies, and enhancing provider capacity."

www.vynca.org

People in the Oregon Health and Science University, who have over 25 years of experience with POLST, offer easy-to-follow advice on navigating the complexities of advance-care planning.

25 Discussion Points for Book Groups

1. What do you feel are the wrongs, real or imagined, in Sandy's case?

2. If you were in a position to right the wrongs, what would you do? Which ones would you give the highest priority?

3. What do you feel Sandy's legacy is? To what extent does it have meaning to people outside her friends and family?

4. People in The Hospice told Larry and Meredith that, in advocating for Sandy's right to die, they had given her a gift. Do you agree? If you had been in their position, what would you have done?

5. Both Larry and Helen speak of Sandy as a child of Holocaust survivors. How do you think that experience affected her life?

6. Would Chapter 1 ("The Goodbye") be better placed in chronological sequence after Chapter 3 ("The Emails")? Why do you think Larry chose to start the book as he did? From your perspective, how important is it to have the opportunity to say goodbye to a loved one?

7. What, if anything, do the texts between Larry and Meredith reveal about their relationship with Sandy and each other? How, if at all, does the father-daughter relationship change? Is it for the better?

8. Do you think Larry was right to share information about Sandy's condition with friends and family members in real time, instead of keeping it private as Sandy might have preferred? Why or why not?

9. What do you think of the funeral and the speakers who tried to capture Sandy's life? What themes were common? Which individual thoughts were revealing? Why?

10. When do you think the grieving process started for Larry? Based on your own experiences, what advice would you have given him?

11. There are no "shoulds" in grieving, in that everyone has to do what works for his or her personality. Yet, based on his behavior, Larry developed certain practices to guide him through the grieving process. What were they? Do you feel he will be successful in moving forward?

12. What do Ellyn's letter, Bria's note, and the actions of Dana and Linda from Papyrus have in common? How do they compare to TBTF's institutional response? In the grieving process, can random acts of kindness supplant impersonal bureaucratic actions? Do you feel it was wise for Larry to challenge TBTF's corporate culture? Explain.

13. Can you describe examples of institutional insensitivity you may have experienced in dealing with a loss? In grieving over a loss, have you experienced unexpected acts of kindness? Explain.

14. How did Sandy's treatment in The Hospital compare to her treatment at The Hospice? Explain the difference.

15. Larry tried to meticulously document what happened. Why do you feel he needed to keep this record? In Chapter 6 ("A Memory"), Jeanette has to prompt Larry to recall a conversation with Sandy. Why didn't he include that conversation in his original documentation?

16. Are memories malleable? Do you have a memory of a lost loved one that has changed over time?

17. What lessons should Americans learn from Sandy's death? Do we treat people approaching the end of life with dignity and respect? Explain based on your own experiences.

18. Do you and your loved ones have an advance directive? Why or why not? Were there any practical ideas that might help you or a loved one plan his or her end-of-life experience? Are there other resources you know of which could be helpful?

19. The Institute of Medicine, which published a report on "Dying in America," hopes it will change the way Americans receive end-of-life care. Given America's

political climate, do you feel they that will be successful in bringing about needed changes? Why or why not?

20. If you had the power to wave your hand and to improve end-of-life care by law or regulation, what would that look like? Are there things you can or should do to help foster such changes in your community and beyond? Explain.

21. Charlie, at age seven and a half, was given a memory box to channel her feelings about the loss of her grandmother. What is one image of Sandy you would like to tell Charlie she should include in her memory box?

22. Dexter, now three years old, will barely remember his grandmother. This book is as much for him as it is for Charlie. What type of planning is necessary for you to create a legacy about a loved one so it can be passed down to future generations?

23. Larry proposes that prophylactic suicide, if widely accepted, would be a "game changer" and allow people in America to have a good death. Do you agree or disagree? Why or why not?

24. In the epilogue, months after Sandy's death, Larry experiences a "flash remembrance" when reading an article in the paper. Have you experienced a "flash remembrance" after the death of a loved one, and if so, what triggered it? How would you describe the experience?

25. Larry thought carefully about how to end the book. Why did he do so by describing a dinner with Meredith? What do you think the last sentence of the epilogue means?

Join the Conversation

www.thegrievancebook.com

THE GRIEVANCE — Lawrence Abrams

Acknowledgments

I WOULD LIKE to acknowledge the reader of this book as the most important part of the equation to change our end-of-life system. I chose to publish the book myself in order to have control of the final copy and distribution. I am more interested in getting this story into the hands of people who can make a difference than I am in profiting from the work. If readers understand the different levels in this story, and then compare and contrast them to their own life experiences, I believe change is possible. Whatever conversations you choose to have and whatever actions you choose to take, they need to start someplace. My earnest hope is that this book will be a catalyst to help people think clearly about end-of-life issues.

At The Hospital and throughout the grieving process, I tried my best to be open to the kindness of professional staff members, friends, acquaintances, and even strangers. Their random and often extraordinary acts of kindness have coalesced in my thoughts and compelled me to advocate for a better end-of-life system.

I write in a very collaborative style, often giving either raw segments of my work or conversations about literary ideas to people for feedback. I listen carefully to them and do many revisions until I feel my writing is the best it can be. The people involved in this collaboration included, especially, my daughter, Meredith, without whose support the book never

174

would have been written. Our understanding of each other's thoughts and needs is what every father-daughter relationship should be about. My grandchildren, Charlie and Dexter, in their innocence, gave me the perseverance to reach out beyond myself and create a written legacy. My son-in-law, Drew, helped me electronically process the manuscript with ease.

I thank Barbara Weinstein, who knew when and how to tell me that I needed to be less self-indulgent and more focused on the book's positive mission. Her husband, Lou Bernstein, a lawyer who writes as well as he speaks, corrected certain passages. In addition, Erich Bechtel – or "Uncle" Erich, as Charlie calls him – had the foresight to volunteer his mother, Martha DeRight, a court stenographer, who carefully transcribed Chapter 1 ("The Goodbye") from an iPhone recording.

My sincere thanks to Phil Tama and Ellyn Toscano, who read early drafts and saw power in my writing but challenged me to find a larger purpose that would encourage people to read the book on multiple levels; to Lenny and Sherry Levine, who knew how to tune into the sensitivity in my writing and to crystallize my experience in the grieving process; to Sherry's sister, Carolyn Wells, who has the clinical training and common sense to understand my journey based on her experience; to Jeanette and Carl Katz, who read early drafts of the work, which Jeanette then networked to nurture me along. (As Jeanette is a nurturer, so is Carl – but in the "strong and silent type" way.)

Our friends Alice and Max Neufeld expressed such powerful empathy that their support will never be forgotten. I am similarly grateful to Steve Feldman and his wife, Libby, who had remarkable insight into my voyage during the grieving process, and to Dr. Steve Tarnoff and his wife, Anne, who after reading a segment of the book focused me on one essential question: What do I want hospitals to do better?

I also thank John Ciarelli, one of my oldest friends, who read the entire manuscript and who not only gave me the most succinct grieving advice *(Larry, just snap out of it)*, but also gave me thoughtful legal advice. My thanks, too, to Carolyn Ciarelli, John's wife, for her compassion – and for a retort *(John, how can you say that?)*; and to Sarah Boonin, who read the entire manuscript and was able to help me understand my own frustrations, in addition to the difference between malpractice and ill treatment, and who guided me to make sensible choices.

And I am grateful to Fran and Bob Boonin, Sarah's parents, and to Carole and Stu London, Bria and Cienna's grandparents, who enveloped me in a safety net where I could freely share my feelings of loss. Jill and Adam London, to quote Jill, "stepped into my circle" with great kindness. The Sigelakis family understood the loss and helped me recover. Both of my therapists, Mary Kay King of the Visiting Nurse Service and Lois Akner at the 92nd Street Y, showed me the healing power of therapy and the ability to sense when the time was right to leave.

Ellen Victor, Marie Viola, and Jodie Cohen, professional and personal friends of Sandy and me, were extraordinary in eulogizing Sandy in a way nobody else could. My cousin Julian and his wife, Rochelle, met with me every week or so to give me a venue in which to express my ideas and then refine them in our conversations. My niece Jennifer Klimko, my nephew Jeremy Abrams, and their respective families helped me through the difficult times by reinforcing the value of family. Helen Adler and her husband, Elliot, made me aware of the power my writing might have in therapy and in promoting end-of-life issues to a larger audience.

Two couples, Patti Schulte and Tom Yamin, and Carolyn Weiss and Bob Jacobson, helped me understand that it was possible to be happy in a relationship again if you are in your 60s and suddenly find yourself alone. Their stories gave me hope that while I never will be able to replace Sandy, I can find both love and companionship. After all, they did. Bob, a retired editor and writer, honed the manuscript with precision and sensitivity, and helped me prepare it for publication.

Dr. Stephanie Pincus, my new neighbor, did not know Sandy. She read the entire manuscript and, having previously helped to organize the Institute of Medicine's "Dying in America" study committee, gave me valuable technical feedback. Tom Schalk, my financial advisor at Merrill, became much more than that during the grieving process. He became a friend whose knowledge helped me through this transition and afforded me the time and finances needed to complete this work.

Leo Weiss, Sandy's cousin from Montreal, and his wife, Marilyn, reawakened my sense of extended family and, with humor, helped me focus on what is important in this life. To quote Marilyn, who is a golfer, "I know I am fine as long as I am vertical and walking on top of the greens as opposed to being horizontal and lying underneath them." I also wish to thank Jason Rehmus for his editing contribution, and Teresa Lagerman (www.mimoYmima.com) for her creative work on the cover.

Above all, a wonderful network of family and friends wrapped me in a cocoon, some with a single strand of silk and others with meticulously interwoven fibers. Each strand and fiber of the cocoon's structure helped me grow and become strong again. I will be forever grateful.